THE Anti-Inflammatory Diet for Beginners 2025

Copyright

all right reserve.no part of this publication may be reproduced, distributed or transmitted in any form or by any means, including photocopying , recording or other electronics, mechanical method, without the prior written permission of the publisher except in the case of brief quotations embodied in critical reviews certain other non commercial use permitted by copyright law

copyright ©Clara Ribeiro Costa, **2024**

Table of Contents

Part I: Understanding Inflammation & Nutrition

1. Introduction to the Anti-Inflammatory Lifestyle

2. The Science of Chronic Inflammation

3. Foods to Embrace and Avoid

4. Health Benefits of the Anti-Inflammatory Diet

5. Key Spices and Supplements for Fighting Inflammation

6. Building a Balanced Anti-Inflammatory Plate

Part II: Meal Planning Made Easy
7. Pantry Staples and Grocery Shopping Tips
8. Batch Cooking and Meal Prep Essentials
9. 7-Day Meal Plan Overview
10. Adapting the Diet to Your Lifestyle (Gluten-Free, Vegan, and More)

Part III: 50 Easy and Delicious Anti-Inflammatory Recipes

Breakfasts

1. Turmeric Oatmeal with Blueberries

2. Avocado Toast on Sprouted-Grain Bread

3. Green Smoothie with Spinach and Chia Seeds

4. Coconut Yogurt with Berries and Almonds

5. Cinnamon-Roll Overnight Oats

Snacks & Smoothies

6. Golden Milk Smoothie

7. Roasted Chickpeas with Sea Salt

8. Trail Mix with Nuts, Seeds, and Dark Chocolate

9. Apple Slices with Almond Butter

10. Hummus with Veggie Sticks

Salads & Soups

11. Quinoa and Kale Salad with Lemon-Tahini Dressing

12. Lentil Soup with Spinach

13. Roasted Beet and Arugula Salad

14. Cucumber and Avocado Salads

15. Tomato Gazpacho

Mains: Plant-Based

16. Buddha Bowl with Tofu and Brown Rice

17. Mushroom and Lentil Tacos

18. Chickpea and Sweet Potato Curry

19. Zucchini Noodles with Pesto

20. Stuffed Bell Peppers

Mains: Fish & Poultry

21. Baked Salmon with Lemon and Dill

22. Herbed Cod with Roasted Tomatoes

23. Chicken Stir-Fry with Broccoli

24. Grilled Tuna Salad with Avocado

25. Turmeric Chicken with Quinoa

Vegetables & Sides

26. Roasted Brussels Sprouts with Balsamic Glaze

27. Steamed Asparagus with Olive Oil

28. Sweet Potato Fries

29. Cauliflower Rice Pilaf

30. Sautéed Spinach with Garlic

Desserts & Treats

31. Chia Seed Pudding with Mango

32. Dark Chocolate Almond Bark

33. Baked Apples with Cinnamon

34. Coconut Macaroons

35. Avocado Chocolate Mousse

Part IV: Week-By-Week Meal Plans & Shopping Lists

36. Week 1: Introduction and Simple Meals

37. Week 2: Adding Variety and New Flavors

38. Week 3: Seasonal and Budget-Friendly Ideas

39. Week 4: Advanced Batch Cooking Techniques

Part V: Troubleshooting and Motivation

40. Handling Cravings and Cheat Days

41. Adapting the Diet for Families

42. Common Pitfalls to Avoid

43. Staying Motivated and Tracking Progress

44. Eating Out While Staying on Track

Part VI: Resources & FAQs

45. Recommended Books and Websites

46. Frequently Asked Questions

47. Supplements and Tools to Support Inflammation Management

48. Glossary of Anti-Inflammatory Foods

49. Recipe Index

50. Acknowledgments and About the Author

Sources for Your Research and Meal Ideas

1. Eating Well – Anti-Inflammatory Meal Plans

2. Healthline – 7-Day Meal Plan

3. Verywell Fit – Anti-Inflammatory Eating

4. Harvard Health – Quick-Start Anti-Inflammation Guide

5. Simon & Schuster – Anti-Inflammatory Diet Overview

1• Understanding Inflammation & Nutrition

- Inflammation is a natural process the body uses to protect itself from injury and infection. However, when it becomes chronic, it can silently damage tissues and organs, contributing to diseases like heart conditions, diabetes, arthritis, and even depression. Diet plays a crucial role in either promoting or reducing inflammation, which is why understanding how to nourish your body is essential for long-term well-being.

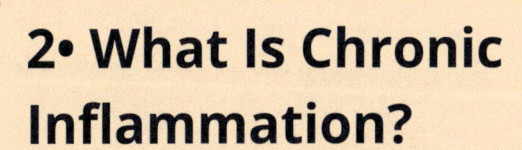

-

2• What Is Chronic Inflammation?

- Acute inflammation is short-term and serves a protective role—like swelling after an injury. In contrast, chronic inflammation occurs when the immune system remains activated for extended periods, even without a direct threat. This constant immune response can harm healthy cells and promote conditions like obesity, Alzheimer's, and autoimmune disorders. The foods we eat often influence how much inflammation lingers in the body.

-

3• What Causes Chronic Inflammation?

- Several factors, including stress, environmental toxins, poor sleep, and lifestyle habits, can trigger chronic inflammation. Processed foods, sugar-laden snacks, and trans fats increase inflammatory markers, contributing to long-term health risks. On the other hand, choosing nutrient-dense foods can help manage or reverse inflammation.

-

9

4• Foods That Fight Inflammation

The anti-inflammatory diet emphasizes whole foods rich in antioxidants, fiber, and healthy fats. Here are a few staples:

• **Leafy Greens:** Kale, spinach, and arugula contain phytonutrients that protect cells.

• **Berries:** Blueberries, strawberries, and raspberries are packed with antioxidants like anthocyanins.

• **Healthy Fats:** Omega-3 in salmon, chia seeds, and walnuts reduce inflammatory markers.

• **Herbs and Spices:** Turmeric and ginger contain compounds like curcumin, which block inflammatory pathways.

• **Fermented Foods:** Yogurt, kimchi, and kombucha promote gut health, which is key to inflammation control.

Foods to Avoid

Some foods are known to increase inflammation over time, such as:

• **Refined Carbohydrates**: White bread, pastries, and sugary cereals spike blood sugar.

• **Red and Processed Meats:** Bacon, sausages, and other cured meats can elevate inflammatory proteins.

• **Fried Foods and Trans Fats:** Found in fast foods and baked goods, these increase oxidative stress.

• **Sugary Drinks:** Soda and energy drinks promote insulin resistance, a driver of inflammation.

5• Health Benefits of Reducing Inflammation

Switching to an anti-inflammatory diet can bring significant improvements in health. It helps regulate blood sugar, lower cholesterol, reduce joint pain, and improve digestion. Over time, this way of eating can enhance energy levels, support weight loss, and even boost mental clarity. Individuals with autoimmune conditions or chronic pain often report relief from their symptoms after adopting anti-inflammatory nutrition.

6• Spices and Supplements for Added Support

Beyond food choices, certain spices and supplements offer anti-inflammatory benefits. Turmeric, thanks to curcumin, can relieve joint pain, while ginger eases digestive inflammation. Omega-3 supplements are effective at lowering inflammation in people who don't consume enough fish. Green tea, rich in polyphenols, is another potent anti-inflammatory agent.

Building a Balanced Plate for Daily Wellness

A balanced anti-inflammatory meal is easy to create with a few guiding principles. Fill half your plate with vegetables (like broccoli or leafy greens), add a quarter of lean protein (such as fish or tofu), and the remaining quarter with whole grains or healthy fats (like quinoa or avocado). Emphasize diversity by incorporating colorful vegetables and fruits to maximize your nutrient intake. Eating mindfully—slowing down and savoring each bite—further supports digestion and reduces stress, which can amplify inflammation if left unchecked.

This approach isn't a rigid diet but a flexible lifestyle that encourages long-term change. The goal is sustainability: focusing on foods that nurture your body, while minimizing those that undermine health. With consistency, adopting anti-inflammatory nutrition can lead to better immunity, fewer aches and pains, and a sense of vitality that radiates from the inside out.

Part II: Meal Planning Made Easy

1•Pantry Staples and Grocery Shopping Tips

A well-stocked pantry is the cornerstone of a healthy, anti-inflammatory lifestyle. It ensures you always have nutritious ingredients on hand to create quick, satisfying meals, even on busy days. The key is to focus on whole foods with a long shelf life, versatile enough for multiple recipes. Below is a guide to building your pantry, along with grocery shopping strategies to stay organized and on budget.

•Essential Pantry Staples for Anti-Inflammatory Cooking

These staples are grouped into categories to simplify shopping and preparation. They'll help you avoid processed foods while supporting vibrant, nutrient-rich meals.

1. Whole Grains and Legumes

- Quinoa: High in fiber and protein, perfect for salads and bowls.
- Oats: Ideal for breakfast or baking, packed with botanical to lower inflammation.
- Lentils & Chickpeas: Great in soups, curries, or roasted as snacks.
- Brown Rice: A fiber-rich side or base for stir-fries.

2. Healthy Fats and Oils

- **Extra Virgin Olive Oil:** Use for dressings and low-heat cooking.
- **Avocado Oil:** Perfect for high-heat cooking.
Nuts & Seeds (Walnuts, Chia, Flaxseeds): Add crunch to salads or smoothies.
- **Nut Butters:** Almond or cashew butter for snacks or sauces.

3. Canned and Jarred Items

- **Canned Fish (Salmon, Sardines):** Excellent sources of Omega-3 s.
- **Tomatoes (Diced or Pureed):** Perfect for sauces and stews.
- **Coconut Milk:** Adds richness to soups and curries.
- **Vegetable Broth:** Essential for quick soups and braising vegetables.

4. Herbs, Spices, and Flavor Enhancers

- **Turmeric & Ginger:** Powerhouses for reducing inflammation.
- **Cinnamon & Cloves:** Add to both sweet and savory dishes.
- **Garlic & Onion Powder:** Build layers of flavor without extra sodium.
- **Apple Cider Vinegar:** Useful in dressings and marinades.

5. Fermented Foods and Probiotic Boosters

- **Sauerkraut or Kimchi:** Supports gut health.
- **Miso Paste:** Adds umami to soups and dressings.

Grocery Shopping Tips for Success

1. Plan Meals in Advance
Start with a basic meal plan for the week, listing out breakfasts, lunches, dinners, and snacks. Make sure your shopping list reflects these planned meals to avoid unnecessary purchases.

2. Organize Your List by Store Sections
Divide your grocery list into sections—produce, pantry staples, proteins, dairy, and frozen items. This helps you shop efficiently and reduces the temptation to stray into less healthy aisles

3. Shop Seasonally for Fresh Produce

Seasonal fruits and vegetables not only taste better but are usually more affordable. Try rotating your produce choices with what's in season to add variety to your meals.

4. Buy in Bulk for Pantry Staples

Items like grains, beans, and nuts are often cheaper in bulk. If possible, store them in airtight containers to keep them fresh for longer. This strategy not only saves money but also reduces packaging waste.

6. Take Advantage of Sales and Loyalty Programs

Many stores offer discounts or loyalty programs for frequent shoppers. Keep an eye out for deals on pantry staples and long-lasting items so you can stock up without overspending.

7. Don't Shop on an Empty Stomach

This may seem obvious, but shopping when hungry can lead to impulse buys, often of less healthy options. Eat a small snack beforehand to help you stay focused on your list.

Maintaining an Organized Pantry

After shopping, group similar items together—grains with grains, spices with spices, and so on. Use clear containers for easy visibility, and place older items in the front to ensure they get used first. Regularly check expiration dates and keep a running list of staples that need replenishing. This small habit ensures you're always ready to whip up nutritious meals without last-minute stress.

A thoughtfully stocked pantry, paired with smart shopping habits, empowers you to make healthier choices effortlessly. By focusing on high-quality ingredients and planning ahead, you'll stay on track with your anti-inflammatory lifestyle while also saving time and money.

2• Batch Cooking and Meal Prep Essentials

Batch cooking and meal prep are game-changers for staying on track with healthy eating. By preparing food in larger quantities and storing it for later use, you minimize cooking time during the week, reduce food waste, and ensure nutritious meals are always available. This system eliminates last-minute decisions, making it easier to avoid processed foods and unhealthy takeout. Below, we'll explore key strategies, tools, and best practices to help you master batch cooking and meal prep.

Why Batch Cooking Works

The idea behind batch cooking is to prepare several servings of foods or entire meals in one session, usually over the weekend or a day off. Whether it's cooking grains in bulk, making soups to freeze, or roasting trays of vegetables, having components ready means meals come together quickly during the week. It's also budget-friendly since you can buy ingredients in larger quantities and avoid frequent grocery trips.

Essential Tools for Meal Prep

- **Glass Storage Containers:** Airtight containers help keep food fresh and allow you to see what's inside easily.
- **Freezer Bags:** Ideal for storing prepped ingredients, sauces, or frozen meals.
- Sheet Pans and Slow Cookers: Great for roasting veggies or making big batches of soups and stews.
- **Mason Jars:** Perfect for salads, overnight oats, or smoothie ingredients.
- **Labeling Supplies:** Use labels to note the contents and date to avoid waste and confusion.

What Foods Work Best for Batch Cooking?

Not every food holds up well over time, so it's important to focus on dishes that store and reheat easily. Here are some of the best options for batch cooking:

- **Whole Grains:** Quinoa, brown rice, and farro can be made in large quantities and stored for sides or grain bowls.
- **Roasted Vegetables:** Sweet potatoes, Brussels sprouts, and carrots stay flavorful for several days
- **Proteins:** Grilled chicken, baked salmon, tofu, or boiled eggs are easy to prepare in batches.
- **Soups, Stews, and Curries:** These improve in flavor over time and freeze well for future meals.
- **Sauces and Dressings:** Homemade hummus, pesto, or vinaigrettes last for a week and elevate simple dishes.

Planning Your Prep Sessions

1. Select Recipes and Build a Prep List

Start by choosing a few meals to focus on. Aim for diversity—perhaps a grain bowl, a soup, a pasta dish, and a breakfast option. List all the ingredients needed and organize them by category (produce, pantry items, etc.).

2. Prep Smart by Grouping Tasks

Think in terms of tasks, not recipes. For example, chop all vegetables at once, cook multiple grains together, and use your oven efficiently by roasting several trays at the same time. If a slow cooker is part of your plan, let it run while you complete other tasks.

3. Work in Stages

If you're tight on time, break meal prep into stages. Day one could involve washing and chopping produce, day two might focus on cooking grains and proteins, and the final day can be assembling meals or packing them into containers.

How to Keep It Interesting

Eating the same meal repeatedly can lead to boredom, so include variety in your batch cooking by using adaptable ingredients. For example, grilled chicken can go into wraps one day and grain bowls the next. Change up seasonings or sauces to transform leftovers into new dishes. You can also build flexibility into your prep by prepping components rather than full meals—like pre-cooked grains, roasted veggies, and a few proteins—to mix and match throughout the week.

Batch cooking and meal prep are invaluable strategies for anyone aiming to eat well without daily hassle. With a little organization, the right tools, and a focus on versatile ingredients, you can ensure that healthy meals are always within reach. Over time, this routine not only saves time and money but also makes it much easier to stick to your dietary goals and enjoy nourishing food, even on your busiest days.

Storage Tips to Maximize Freshness

- **Cool Foods Completely:** Always let food cool before sealing it in containers to prevent condensation, which can cause spoilage.

- **Use the Freezer Wisely:** Soups, sauces, and pre-portioned meals store well in the freezer for weeks or months.

- **Practice FIFO (First In, First Out):** Arrange prepped meals so that older items are used first, preventing waste.

- **Separate Wet and Dry Ingredients:** For salads and grain bowls, store dressings separately to keep them from getting soggy.

3• 7-Day Meal Plan Overview

This 7-day anti-inflammatory meal plan is designed to provide balance, variety, and ease of preparation. It emphasizes nutrient-dense foods, such as vegetables, lean proteins, whole grains, healthy fats, and anti-inflammatory herbs and spices. Each day includes three main meals and snacks, ensuring you stay energized while reducing inflammation naturally. Below is a breakdown of what your week could look like.

Day 1

- **Breakfast:** Overnight oats with chia seeds, berries, and almond milk.
- **Lunch:** Quinoa salad with avocado, cherry tomatoes, cucumber, and lemon vinaigrette.
- **Dinner:** Baked salmon with roasted asparagus and sweet potatoes.
- **Snack:** Handful of walnuts and green tea.

Day 2

- **Breakfast:** Green smoothie with spinach, banana, chia seeds, and plant-based protein powder.
- **Lunch:** Lentil soup with mixed greens on the side.
- **Dinner:** Stir-fried tofu with broccoli, bell peppers, and brown rice.
- **Snack:** Hummus with sliced cucumbers and carrots.

Day 3

- **Breakfast:** Chia pudding topped with mango and coconut flakes.
- **Lunch:** Roasted vegetable and quinoa bowl with tahini dressing.
- **Dinner:** Grilled chicken with sauteed zucchini and wild rice.
- **Snack:** Apple slices with almond butter.

Day 4

- **Breakfast:** Oatmeal with cinnamon, blueberries, and flaxseeds.
- **Lunch:** Avocado toast on whole grain bread with arugula and poached egg.
- **Dinner:** Turmeric chickpea curry over basmati rice.
- **Snack:** Dark chocolate (85%) and a handful of almonds.

Day 5

• **Breakfast:** Scrambled eggs with sauteed spinach and whole-grain toast.

• **Lunch**: Greek salad with olives, cucumbers, tomatoes, and grilled shrimp.

• Dinner: Baked cod with roasted Brussels sprouts and quinoa.

• Snack: A small bowl of mixed berries.

Day 6

• Breakfast: Smoothie bowl with banana, berries, chia seeds, and granola.

• Lunch: Falafel wrap with hummus, tomatoes, and leafy greens.

• Dinner: Turkey meatballs with zucchini noodles and marinara sauce.

• Snack: Roasted chickpeas with sea salt and paprika.

Day 7

• Breakfast: Whole-grain waffles topped with almond butter and strawberries.

Lunch: Grilled vegetable wrap with hummus and mixed greens.

Dinner: Black bean tacos with avocado, salsa, and a side of sautéed kale.

Snack: Coconut yogurt with sliced kiwi and chia seeds.

How to Make It Work

Batch cooking: Prepare larger portions of grains, soups, or proteins early in the week to save time.

Flexibility: Mix and match meals to suit your preferences and use what you have on hand.

Snack smart: Keep healthy snacks available to curb cravings between meals.

Stay hydrated: Drink plenty of water or herbal tea throughout the day to support digestion and overall well-being.

This plan offers a practical framework to reduce inflammation without sacrificing flavor or variety. Use it as a starting point, adjusting portions and ingredients based on your lifestyle and needs.

4 • ADAPTING THE DIET TO YOUR LIFESTYLE (GLUTEN-FREE, VEGAN, AND MORE)

Adapting an anti-inflammatory diet to fit your lifestyle—whether gluten-free, vegan, or tailored for other needs—requires a thoughtful approach. The key is to honor your personal preferences while staying committed to the principles of whole, minimally processed foods. Below are strategies for integrating various dietary adjustments without compromising on taste, variety, or nutrition.

Gluten-Free Adaptations

• For those avoiding gluten, the goal is to replace common grains with alternatives that align with the anti-inflammatory approach. Swap wheat-based items with:

• Quinoa, Brown Rice, Buckwheat: Naturally gluten-free grains packed with fiber and essential nutrients.

• Gluten-Free Oats: Perfect for breakfasts or baking.

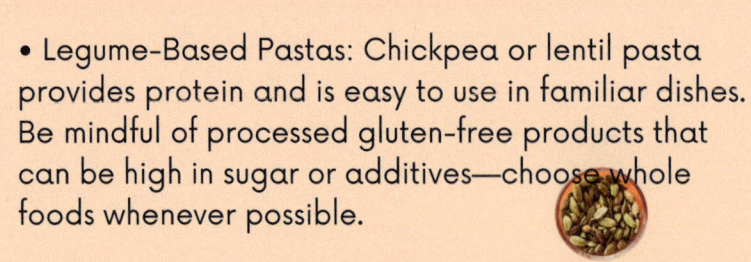

• Legume-Based Pastas: Chickpea or lentil pasta provides protein and is easy to use in familiar dishes. Be mindful of processed gluten-free products that can be high in sugar or additives—choose whole foods whenever possible.

Vegan and Plant-Based Adjustments

A vegan lifestyle works seamlessly with anti-inflammatory principles when you prioritize whole, plant-based ingredients. Focus on:

24

- Legumes and Tofu: Replace animal proteins with chickpeas, lentils, black beans, and tofu.

- Nuts, Seeds, and Nut Butters: Almonds, flaxseeds, and tahini are excellent sources of healthy fats and protein.

- Leafy Greens and Colorful Vegetables: Spinach, kale, and cruciferous vegetables offer antioxidants and fiber.

Ensure you meet your vitamin B12, iron, and omega-3 needs by including fortified foods, nutritional yeast, or algae-based supplements.

Pescatarian or Flexitarian Variations

For those who prefer a flexible diet, incorporating fish or occasional animal products provides additional options.

- Fatty Fish (Salmon, Sardines): Rich in omega-3 fatty acids, which fight inflammation.

- Eggs and Greek Yogurt: Provide high-quality protein and probiotics.
- Balance animal-based meals with plant-based sides, ensuring most of your plate consists of vegetables and whole grains.

Managing Multiple Restrictions (Soy-Free, Nut-Free, Etc.)

- If you have other dietary concerns, such as avoiding soy or nuts, creativity becomes essential.

- Soy-Free Proteins: Opt for legumes, hemp seeds, and quinoa as plant-based protein sources.

- Nut-Free Fats: Avocados, olive oil, and sunflower seeds make excellent substitutes.

Look for allergen-friendly recipes that use simple, whole ingredients to avoid over-relying on processed alternatives.

Making the Diet Sustainable for You

The most effective dietary changes are the ones you can sustain over time. Adapt the plan to fit your routine and preferences:

• Batch Cook Versatile Components: Prepare grains, roasted vegetables, and dressings to mix and match for meals.

• Include Flex Days: Build in days to enjoy your favorite foods, whether dining out or experimenting in the kitchen.
• Stay mindful of how your body responds to different foods, adjusting the plan as needed to maintain both enjoyment and health benefits.

Adapting the anti-inflammatory diet to your lifestyle is all about finding what works for you while staying grounded in whole, nourishing foods. Whether you're gluten-free, vegan, or simply trying to eat more mindfully, this diet can evolve with you, offering flexibility without sacrificing its core health benefits.

Part III: 50 Easy and Delicious Anti-Inflammatory Recipes

A• Breakfasts

1. Turmeric Oatmeal with Blueberries

Turmeric Oatmeal with Blueberries

Turmeric oatmeal with blueberries is a powerhouse breakfast that combines anti-inflammatory ingredients with natural sweetness. The base of this dish is rolled oats, a slow-digesting grain that keeps you full and stabilizes blood sugar levels. Turmeric, known for its curcumin content, adds a warming, earthy flavor while promoting reduced inflammation. Black pepper is often added to enhance curcumin absorption.

How to Prepare:

1. Cook the Oats: Simmer oats with plant-based milk or water for a creamy texture.

2. Add Spices: Stir in a teaspoon of turmeric, a pinch of cinnamon, and black pepper for depth of flavor.

3. Sweeten Naturally: Use a drizzle of honey or maple syrup.

4. Top with Blueberries: Add fresh or frozen blueberries to boost antioxidants.

5. Optional Toppings: Almonds, chia seeds, or a dollop of almond butter for healthy fats.

2. Avocado Toast on Sprouted-Grain Bread

Avocado toast on sprouted-grain bread is a nourishing, flavorful meal that fits perfectly into an anti-inflammatory diet. Sprouted-grain bread offers more fiber, vitamins, and minerals compared to traditional bread, as the sprouting process enhances nutrient absorption. Paired with creamy avocado, this dish delivers a rich dose of healthy fats, fiber, and antioxidants, helping to support heart health and stabilize blood sugar levels.

How to Make It:

1. Toast the Bread: Use sprouted-grain bread for extra nutrients and a crunchy texture.

2. Prepare the Avocado: Mash half an avocado with a pinch of salt, pepper, and a drizzle of olive oil. Optionally, add lemon juice for brightness.

3. Assemble: Spread the avocado on the toasted bread.

4. Customize with Toppings:

• **Tomato and Basil:** Adds freshness and antioxidants.

• **Red Pepper Flakes or Chili Oil:** For a spicy kick.

• **Hemp Seeds or Microgreens:** Boost nutrition with extra fiber and antioxidants.

This versatile dish works for breakfast, a quick snack, or even a light lunch. The healthy fats from avocado provide lasting satiety, while the sprouted grains give sustained energy.

3. Green Smoothie with Spinach and Chia Seeds

A green smoothie with spinach and chia seeds is a nutrient-packed option to jumpstart your day or provide an energy boost. Spinach, rich in vitamins A, C, and K, provides antioxidants and essential minerals, while chia seeds deliver omega-3 fatty acids, fiber, and protein for lasting fullness. This smoothie is also easily adaptable to various tastes and dietary needs.

How to Prepare:

1. Blend the Base: Combine 1 cup of unsweetened almond milk or water with a handful of spinach

2. Add Fruit: Include half a banana and some pineapple or mango for natural sweetness.

3. Incorporate Chia Seeds: Add 1 tablespoon of chia seeds for fiber and healthy fats.

4. Boost Flavor and Nutrition: Optional ingredients include ginger, fresh mint, or a scoop of plant-based protein powder.

5. Blend Until Smooth: Ensure the mixture is creamy and well-blended. You can also add ice for a chilled texture.

This smoothie provides a perfect blend of hydration, fiber, vitamins, and minerals. It helps reduce inflammation and supports digestion, while the chia seeds promote sustained energy throughout the day. Best of all, it's versatile—you can swap fruits or add other superfoods, such as flaxseeds or avocado, to meet your preferences.

4. Coconut Yogurt with Berries and Almonds

Coconut yogurt with berries and almonds is a refreshing, nutrient-dense option that works well for breakfast, a snack, or even dessert. Coconut yogurt provides healthy fats and probiotics, which support digestion and gut health. Unlike dairy-based yogurt, it's naturally free from lactose, making it ideal for those on a plant-based or dairy-free diet.

How to Prepare:

1. Base: Start with plain, unsweetened coconut yogurt to avoid added sugars.

2. Add Fresh Berries: Use blueberries, strawberries, or raspberries for natural sweetness and antioxidants.

3. Incorporate Almonds: Top with a handful of raw or lightly toasted almonds for crunch, healthy fats, and protein.

4. Optional Enhancements: Drizzle with honey or maple syrup for extra sweetness, or sprinkle chia seeds for more fiber and Omega-3.

This dish offers a perfect balance of textures and flavors while supporting your body's anti-inflammatory needs. The combination of probiotics, antioxidants, and healthy fats promotes gut health, immunity, and long-lasting energy.

5. Cinnamon-Roll Overnight Oats

Cinnamon-roll overnight oats offer a delightful way to enjoy the flavors of a classic cinnamon roll without the added sugar and refined flour. This recipe combines hearty oats with warm spices and wholesome ingredients, creating a balanced meal that promotes sustained energy and reduces inflammation.

How to Prepare:

1. Combine Ingredients: In a jar or bowl, mix ½ cup of rolled oats, 1 tablespoon of chia seeds, 1 teaspoon of cinnamon, and a pinch of nutmeg.

2. Add Liquid: Pour in ¾ cup of almond milk or your favorite plant-based milk, ensuring the oats are fully submerged.

3. Sweeten Naturally: Add a drizzle of maple syrup or honey for sweetness.

4. Optional Add-ons: Stir in a spoonful of almond butter or vanilla extract for a richer flavor.

B• Snacks & Smoothies

1• Golden Milk Smoothie

A golden milk smoothie combines the soothing properties of traditional turmeric latte with the refreshing elements of a smoothie. Turmeric, the star ingredient, is known for its anti-inflammatory benefits thanks to curcumin. Blending it with creamy plant-based milk and natural sweeteners creates a nourishing, easy-to-digest drink ideal for breakfast or a post-workout snack.

How to Make It:

1. **Base Ingredients**: Add 1 cup of almond or coconut milk to a blender.

2. **Turmeric and Spices**: Include 1 teaspoon of turmeric, ½ teaspoon of cinnamon, and a pinch of black pepper (to aid curcumin absorption).

3. **Sweetener:** Use 1 pitted date or a drizzle of honey.

4. **Fruit for Creaminess:** Add half a frozen banana or mango for a smooth texture.

5. **Optional Add-ons:** A scoop of protein powder or a dash of ginger enhances flavor and nutrition.

6. **Blend Until Smooth:** Ensure the mixture is creamy. Add ice if a chilled texture is preferred

This smoothie delivers an antioxidant boost while also aiding digestion and reducing inflammation. The blend of spices offers not only warmth but also metabolic benefits, making it both soothing and energizing.

2• Roasted Chickpeas with Sea Salt

Roasted chickpeas with sea salt are a crunchy, satisfying snack that fits perfectly into an anti-inflammatory diet. High in protein, fiber, and complex carbohydrates, chickpeas provide sustained energy while promoting gut health. Roasting them creates a crispy texture that makes them a great alternative to processed snacks.

How to Prepare:

1. **Preheat the Oven:** Set to 400°F (200°C).

2. **Rinse and Dry:** Drain and rinse a can of chickpeas. Pat dry with a paper towel to ensure crispiness.

3. **Season:** Toss the chickpeas with 1 tablespoon of olive oil and sea salt. Optional spices include smoked paprika, cumin, or garlic powder for extra flavor.

4. **Roast**: Spread them in a single layer on a baking sheet and roast for 20–30 minutes, shaking the pan halfway through for even browning.

5. Cool and Enjoy: Let them cool completely to achieve maximum crunch.

This simple snack offers a healthy balance of protein and fiber while reducing cravings for less nutritious foods. It's versatile enough to enjoy on its own or as a salad topper. The combination of olive oil and sea salt enhances the natural flavor without overpowering it, making these chickpeas both delicious and wholesome.

3• Trail Mix with Nuts, Seeds, and Dark Chocolate

Trail mix with nuts, seeds, and dark chocolate is a nutrient-dense snack ideal for curbing cravings and providing sustained energy. It combines healthy fats, protein, fiber, and antioxidants, making it a smart choice for anyone following an anti-inflammatory diet. The variety of textures and flavors makes this mix both delicious and functional, supporting heart health, brain function, and stable blood sugar levels.

How to Prepare:

1. Choose the Nuts: Use a mix of almonds, walnuts, or cashews for a blend of protein and omega-3 fats.

2. Add Seeds: Pumpkin seeds and sunflower seeds contribute magnesium and zinc, promoting relaxation and immunity.

3. Incorporate Dried Fruit: Include unsweetened cranberries or raisins for natural sweetness.

4. Dark Chocolate Chunks: Opt for 70% or higher cacao for antioxidants and a touch of indulgence.

5. Optional Add-Ins: Coconut flakes, goji berries, or granola can enhance flavor and variety.

This trail mix offers both portability and flexibility. You can tailor it to your preferences by swapping in different nuts or seeds, and it's an excellent snack to keep on hand for busy days or outdoor activities. The combination of protein, fiber, and healthy fats ensures that it not only satisfies hunger but also promotes long-term health.

33

4• Apple Slices with Almond Butter

Apple slices with almond butter offer a simple yet nourishing snack, perfect for satisfying hunger between meals. This combination delivers a balance of carbohydrates from the apples and healthy fats, protein, and fiber from the almond butter, keeping you energized and satiated. Apples also provide antioxidants and soluble fiber, which aid digestion, while almond butter adds vitamin E and magnesium, supporting heart health.

How to Prepare:

1. Slice the Apple: Choose a crisp apple variety like Fuji or Granny Smith for a refreshing crunch.

2. Spread Almond Butter: Use about 1-2 tablespoons of natural almond butter (without added sugars or oils).

3. Optional Toppings: Sprinkle cinnamon for a warming flavor or chia seeds for added Omega-3.

This snack is versatile and easy to prepare, offering a quick solution for those aiming to maintain steady blood sugar levels and curb cravings in a nutritious way.

5• Hummus with Veggie Sticks

Hummus with veggie sticks is a delightful and nutritious snack that combines the creamy richness of hummus with the crunch of fresh vegetables. This pairing is not only delicious but also offers a host of health benefits, making it a perfect addition to an anti-inflammatory diet. Hummus, primarily made from chickpeas, is rich in protein and fiber, while the variety of veggies contributes essential vitamins and minerals.

How to Prepare:

1. Choose Your Hummus: You can either make your own or buy store-bought varieties. Homemade hummus can be customized with flavors like garlic, roasted red pepper, or spices like cumin and paprika.

2. Select Fresh Vegetables: Cut up a colorful assortment of vegetable sticks, such as carrots, cucumbers, bell peppers, celery, and radishes.

3. Serve: Arrange the veggie sticks around a bowl of hummus for an appealing presentation

This snack is not only visually attractive but also provides a satisfying crunch and creaminess that keeps you full. The fiber in the veggies and the protein in the hummus help maintain energy levels, making it an excellent choice for a mid-afternoon pick-me-up or a light appetizer. Enjoying hummus with veggies is a convenient way to incorporate more plant-based foods into your diet while keeping cravings at bay.

C• Salads & Soups

1• Quinoa and Kale Salad with Lemon-Tahini Dressing

Quinoa and kale salad with lemon-tahini dressing is a vibrant and nutrient-dense dish that brings together the health benefits of whole grains, leafy greens, and a zesty dressing. Quinoa, a complete protein, offers all nine essential amino acids and is packed with fiber, making it a filling base for this salad. Kale adds a hearty texture and a wealth of vitamins A, C, and K, which are essential for overall health.

How to Prepare:

1. Cook the Quinoa: Rinse 1 cup of quinoa under cold water, then cook it in 2 cups of vegetable broth or water according to package instructions. Once cooked, fluff with a fork and let it cool.

2. Prepare the Kale: Remove the tough stems from 4 cups of fresh kale leaves and chop them into bite-sized pieces. Massage the kale with a pinch of salt for a minute to tenderize it.

3. Mix the Ingredients: In a large bowl, combine the cooled quinoa, massaged kale, and any additional mix-ups like cherry tomatoes, diced cucumbers, or avocado for extra flavor and nutrition

4. Make the Dressing: In a separate bowl, whisk together 3 tablespoons of tahini, the juice of 1 lemon, 1 tablespoon of maple syrup, and 1-2 tablespoons of water to achieve your desired consistency. Season with salt and pepper to taste.

5. Combine and Serve: Drizzle the dressing over the salad, toss to combine, and enjoy.

This salad is not only filling but also incredibly versatile. The lemon-tahini dressing provides a creamy, tangy flavor that complements the earthy quinoa and robust kale beautifully. Packed with antioxidants, fiber, and healthy fats, this dish makes for a satisfying lunch or a side dish at dinner, promoting overall wellness and reducing inflammation.

2• Lentil Soup with Spinach

Lentil soup with spinach is a hearty and comforting dish that embodies warmth and nourishment. Packed with protein, fiber, and essential nutrients, this soup is an excellent choice for anyone looking to embrace a healthy, anti-inflammatory diet. Lentils are not only filling but also rich in vitamins and minerals, making them a staple for plant-based diets.

How to Prepare:

1. Sauté Aromatics: Begin by heating 1 tablespoon of olive oil in a large pot over medium heat. Add 1 diced onion, 2 minced garlic cloves, and 1 diced carrot. Sauté until the vegetables soften, about 5 minutes.

2. Add Lentils and Broth: Stir in 1 cup of rinsed lentils and 6 cups of vegetable broth. Bring the mixture to a boil.

3. Season: Add 1 teaspoon of cumin, 1 teaspoon of thyme, and salt and pepper to taste.

4. Simmer: Reduce heat and let it simmer for 25-30 minutes, or until the lentils are tender.

5. Incorporate Spinach: Stir in 4 cups of fresh spinach and cook for an additional 5 minutes until wilted.

6. Finish and Serve: Adjust seasoning if necessary and serve hot, optionally garnished with a squeeze of lemon juice for brightness.

This lentil soup is not just delicious; it also offers a wonderful blend of flavors and textures. The spinach adds a vibrant color and boosts the soup's nutritional profile, making it a wholesome choice for lunch or dinner. Rich in antioxidants and anti-inflammatory compounds, this dish supports overall health while satisfying hunger. Enjoying a bowl can be a comforting way to nourish your body and soul, especially on cooler days.

3• Roasted Beet and Arugula Salads

Roasted beet and arugula salad is a delightful combination of earthy flavors and vibrant colors that not only looks appealing but is also packed with nutrients. Beets are known for their high antioxidant content and anti-inflammatory properties, making them an excellent addition to any meal. Arugula adds a peppery bite and is rich in vitamins A, C, and K, while the overall salad is a fantastic source of fiber.

How to Prepare:

1. Roast the Beets: Preheat your oven to 400°F (200°C). Wrap whole beets in foil and roast for about 45-60 minutes until tender. Once cool, peel and slice them into wedges.

2. Prepare the Arugula: While the beets are roasting, wash and dry about 4 cups of fresh arugula.

3. Make the Dressing: Whisk together 3 tablespoons of olive oil, 1 tablespoon of balsamic vinegar, 1 teaspoon of Dijon mustard, salt, and pepper to taste.

4. Assemble the Salad: In a large bowl, combine the roasted beets and arugula. Drizzle with the dressing and toss gently to combine.

5. Add Extras: For added flavor and texture, sprinkle with crumbled goat cheese or feta, walnuts or pecans, and fresh herbs like parsley or dill.

This salad is versatile and can be served warm or chilled, making it suitable for any season. The sweetness of the beets pairs beautifully with the peppery arugula, while the dressing ties everything together. This dish not only satisfies the palate but also provides an array of health benefits, promoting overall well-being and vibrant health. Enjoy it as a main course or a side dish to elevate your meal.

4• Cucumber and Avocado Salads

Cucumber and avocado salad is a refreshing and nutritious dish that brings together two powerhouse ingredients. Cucumbers are hydrating and low in calories, making them an excellent choice for maintaining a healthy weight. They are rich in vitamins K and C, while avocados provide healthy fats, fiber, and a variety of essential nutrients, including potassium and folate.

How to Prepare:

1. Slice the Cucumbers: Start by washing and slicing 2-3 cucumbers into thin rounds or half-moons. If you prefer, you can peel them for a smoother texture.

2. Prepare the Avocado: Cut 1-2 ripe avocados in half, remove the pit, and scoop the flesh out with a spoon. Dice the avocado into bite-sized pieces.

3. Combine Ingredients: In a large bowl, gently mix the cucumber slices and diced avocado.

4. Dress the Salad: Drizzle with olive oil, the juice of 1 lime or lemon, and sprinkle with salt and pepper to taste. For an extra kick, consider adding minced garlic, fresh herbs like cilantro or parsley, or a pinch of red pepper flakes.

5. Toss and Serve: Gently toss the ingredients to combine, being careful not to mash the avocado. Serve immediately for the best flavor and texture.

This salad is not only quick and easy to prepare but also incredibly versatile. It can be served as a light lunch, a side dish at dinner, or a healthy snack. The creamy avocado complements the crispness of the cucumber beautifully, creating a satisfying contrast. Enjoying this salad regularly can contribute to better hydration, healthy fats, and a range of nutrients that support overall well-being.

5• Tomato Gazpacho

Tomato gazpacho is a chilled Spanish soup that embodies the essence of summer with its refreshing and vibrant flavors. This dish is not only a feast for the eyes but also a nutritious way to enjoy raw vegetables. The base is primarily made from ripe tomatoes, which are rich in vitamins A and C, along with antioxidants that can support overall health and combat inflammation.

How to Prepare:

1. Select the Tomatoes: Choose about 6-8 ripe tomatoes for the best flavor. If possible, use heirloom varieties for added sweetness.

2. Chop the Vegetables: In addition to tomatoes, dice 1 cucumber, 1 bell pepper (red or yellow), and 1 small red onion. Mince 1-2 cloves of garlic for an extra kick.

3. Blend the Base: In a blender, combine the chopped tomatoes, cucumber, bell pepper, onion, and garlic. Blend until smooth. You can adjust the texture by blending less for a chunkier gazpacho.

4. Add Flavor: To enhance the taste, drizzle in 2-3 tablespoons of olive oil, 1-2 tablespoons of red wine vinegar, and season with salt and pepper. For a hint of spice, consider adding a dash of cayenne pepper or hot sauce.

5. Chill: Transfer the soup to a bowl or container and refrigerate for at least 2 hours, allowing the flavors to meld and the gazpacho to become pleasantly chilled.

6. Serve: Serve the gazpacho in bowls, garnished with diced vegetables, fresh herbs like basil or parsley, and a sprinkle of croutons for added texture.

This soup is incredibly versatile and can be customized to your taste. The combination of fresh vegetables creates a refreshing, nutrient-dense dish that's perfect as a light meal or appetizer. Gazpacho is particularly appealing during warm months, as it provides hydration and refreshment. Enjoying this chilled soup not only satisfies your taste buds but also supports your health with every spoonful.

D• Mains: Plant-Based

1• Buddha Bowl with Tofu and Brown Rice

A Buddha bowl with tofu and brown rice is a nourishing and colorful meal that brings together a variety of textures and flavors in one dish. This versatile bowl is an excellent way to incorporate an array of vegetables, protein, and whole grains, making it ideal for a balanced, anti-inflammatory diet. The combination of brown rice and tofu provides complex carbohydrates and plant-based protein, ensuring you feel satisfied and energized.

How to Prepare:

1. Cook the Brown Rice: Begin by rinsing 1 cup of brown rice and cooking it according to package instructions, typically using a ratio of 2 cups of water to 1 cup of rice. Bring to a boil, then reduce to a simmer and cover until tender, about 30-40 minutes.

2. Prepare the Tofu: While the rice is cooking, press 1 block of firm tofu to remove excess moisture. Cut it into cubes and marinate it in a mixture of soy sauce, sesame oil, and your choice of spices like garlic powder or ginger for about 15 minutes.

3. Cook the Tofu: In a skillet over medium heat, add a little oil and cook the marinated tofu until golden and crispy on all sides, about 8-10 minutes.

4. Choose Your Vegetables: Select a mix of fresh and cooked vegetables. Options include steamed broccoli, roasted sweet potatoes, shredded carrots, bell peppers, and sliced cucumbers. Aim for a variety of colors and textures.

5. Assemble the Bowl: In a large bowl, start with a base of brown rice. Arrange the cooked tofu and vegetables on top.

6. Add Dressing: Drizzle your favorite dressing, such as tahini or a simple vinaigrette made with olive oil, lemon juice, salt, and pepper. Garnish with fresh herbs like cilantro or parsley, and sprinkle with seeds or nuts for added crunch.

This Buddha bowl is highly customizable, allowing you to tailor it to your preferences or dietary needs. The combination of wholesome ingredients creates a visually appealing and delicious meal that supports overall health. Enjoying this dish regularly can help maintain energy levels and promote a sense of well-being while satisfying your taste buds with every bite.

2• Mushroom and Lentil Tacos

Mushroom and lentil dishes are a hearty and nutritious combination that celebrates the rich flavors of both ingredients. Lentils are a fantastic source of plant-based protein, fiber, and various vitamins, while mushrooms contribute their unique umami taste along with important nutrients like selenium and B vitamins. This dish is not only satisfying but also versatile, making it an ideal option for a wholesome meal.

How to Prepare:

1. Choose the Lentils: Start by selecting your lentils. Green or brown lentils work well for this dish due to their firm texture. Rinse and soak them for about 30 minutes to help with cooking time.

2. Sauté Aromatics: In a large skillet, heat a tablespoon of olive oil over medium heat. Add one diced onion and sauté until translucent. Incorporating two minced garlic cloves adds an aromatic touch.

3. Cook the Mushrooms: Add 2 cups of sliced mushrooms (such as cremini or button) to the skillet and cook until they release their moisture and become tender, about 5-7 minutes.

4. Combine Ingredients: Stir in the soaked lentils and add 4 cups of vegetable broth. Bring the mixture to a boil, then reduce the heat to a simmer. Cook for 25-30 minutes until the lentils are tender but not mushy.

5. Season: Enhance the flavor with herbs such as thyme or rosemary, along with salt and pepper to taste. A splash of balsamic vinegar or a squeeze of lemon juice can elevate the dish further.

6. Serve: This dish can be enjoyed warm as a main course or served over a bed of greens for a lighter meal. Garnish with fresh parsley or other herbs to add color and freshness.

The earthy flavors of mushrooms combined with the protein-packed lentils create a filling meal that is not only delicious but also supports a healthy lifestyle. This dish is excellent for meal prep, as it keeps well and can be enjoyed over several days, making it a convenient option for busy schedules. With its rich texture and robust taste, mushroom and lentil dishes offer a satisfying and nourishing experience for all palates.

3• Chickpea and Sweet Potato Curry

Chickpea and sweet potato curry is a comforting and nutritious dish that highlights the harmony of flavors from the vibrant spices and wholesome ingredients. This recipe brings together protein-rich chickpeas and fiber-filled sweet potatoes, making it a satisfying meal that nourishes the body and warms the soul. The combination of these ingredients not only supports digestion but also provides a wealth of vitamins and minerals essential for overall health.

How to Prepare:

1. Sauté Aromatics: Start by heating 1 tablespoon of coconut oil in a large pot over medium heat. Add 1 diced onion, 2 minced garlic cloves, and a thumb-sized piece of ginger, grated or minced. Sauté until the onion becomes translucent and fragrant, around 5 minutes.

2. Add Spices: Stir in 1 teaspoon of cumin, 1 teaspoon of coriander, and ½ teaspoon of turmeric or curry powder. Cooking the spices for a minute helps to release their essential oils and intensifies the flavor.

3. Incorporate Vegetables: Add 1 large sweet potato, peeled and diced, and 1 can (15 oz) of drained chickpeas. Mix well to combine with the spices.

4. Pour in Coconut Milk: Add 1 can (13.5 oz) of coconut milk and 1 cup of vegetable broth. Bring the mixture to a gentle boil, then reduce the heat to simmer. Cook for about 20 minutes or until the sweet potatoes are tender.

5. Finish with Greens: Stir in 2 cups of fresh spinach or kale in the last few minutes of cooking until wilted.

6. Season and Serve: Taste and adjust seasoning with salt, pepper, and a squeeze of lime juice to brighten the flavors. Serve the curry warm over rice or quinoa, garnished with fresh cilantro.

This dish not only showcases the delightful combination of sweet and savory flavors but also offers a fantastic balance of nutrients. The creamy coconut milk complements the sweetness of the sweet potatoes, while the chickpeas add a hearty texture. Perfect for a weeknight dinner or meal prep, this chickpea and sweet potato curry is a delightful way to enjoy wholesome ingredients that contribute to a healthier lifestyle. Each spoonful provides comfort and satisfaction, making it a favorite in any kitchen.

4• Zucchini Noodles with Pesto

Zucchini noodles, also known as "zoodles," are a vibrant, low-carb alternative to traditional pasta. This dish offers a refreshing, light meal option while still being rich in flavor thanks to the aromatic pesto sauce. Zucchini is hydrating and nutrient-dense, packed with vitamins A and C, while the pesto provides healthy fats from nuts and olive oil, making this dish a well-rounded choice for a health-conscious lifestyle.

How to Prepare:

1. Spiralize the Zucchini: Use a spiralizer or vegetable peeler to create noodles from 2–3 medium zucchinis. Pat them dry with paper towels to remove excess moisture.

2. Make the Pesto: In a blender or food processor, combine 2 cups of fresh basil leaves, ¼ cup of pine nuts (or walnuts), 2 garlic cloves, ½ cup of olive oil, ½ cup of grated Parmesan (optional), and salt to taste. Blend until smooth.

3. Sauté the Zoodles: Heat a bit of olive oil in a large skillet over medium heat. Add the zucchini noodles and sauté for 2–3 minutes, just until they soften slightly but still retain a bit of crunch.

4. Combine with Pesto: Remove the skillet from heat and toss the warm zucchini noodles with the prepared pesto sauce until well coated.

5. Serve: Garnish with additional Parmesan, pine nuts, or fresh basil. Serve immediately, either on its own or with a side of grilled vegetables or chicken.

This dish is perfect for summer or any time you're craving something light and flavorful. It's easy to customize—swap out pine nuts for almonds, or add cherry tomatoes for extra texture. The result is a satisfying, nutrient-packed meal that is quick to make and delightful to eat. Enjoying zucchini noodles with pesto regularly not only supports a balanced diet but also introduces more fresh vegetables into your routine in a delicious way.

5• Stuffed Bell Peppers

Stuffed bell peppers are a versatile and colorful dish that combines tender peppers with a flavorful filling, creating a perfect blend of textures. The bell peppers act as edible vessels, roasting to a soft, slightly sweet consistency while the filling—typically made with grains, proteins, and vegetables—adds heartiness. This dish works well for both weeknight dinners and meal prep, as it can be customized to suit various dietary preferences.

How to Prepare:

1. Select and Prepare the Peppers: Choose 4–6 large bell peppers of any color. Cut off the tops and remove the seeds and membranes. Brush the peppers lightly with olive oil and set them aside.

2. Prepare the Filling: In a skillet, heat olive oil over medium heat. Sauté 1 diced onion and 2 minced garlic cloves until softened. Add 1 cup of cooked quinoa or brown rice and 1 can (15 oz) of drained black beans or ground turkey. Mix in diced tomatoes, corn, and seasonings like cumin, paprika, salt, and pepper. Simmer for 5–7 minutes until well combined.

3. Stuff the Peppers: Fill the hollowed peppers generously with the prepared mixture. If desired, top with shredded cheese or nutritional yeast for a vegan option.

4. Bake: Place the stuffed peppers in a baking dish and add a little water to the bottom to help steam the peppers. Cover with foil and bake at 375°F (190°C) for 30 minutes. Remove the foil and bake for another 10-15 minutes until the peppers are tender and the filling is heated through.

5. Serve: Garnish with chopped herbs like cilantro or parsley. Serve with a side of salad or avocado slices for added freshness.

This dish offers a delightful combination of sweet, savory, and spiced elements in every bite. With its fiber-rich vegetables and proteins, it's both satisfying and nourishing. Stuffed peppers are adaptable—ingredients like chickpeas, lentils, feta, or mushrooms can easily be swapped in based on your preferences, ensuring a meal that's both delicious and nutrient-dense.

E• Mains: Fish & Poultry

1•Baked Salmon with Lemon and Dill

Baked salmon with lemon and dill is a simple yet elegant dish that balances bright citrus notes with the fresh, earthy aroma of dill. This recipe highlights the natural richness of salmon, providing omega-3 fatty acids and high-quality protein, making it both nourishing and flavorful.

How to Prepare:

1. Preheat the Oven: Set the oven to 375°F (190°C).

2. Prepare the Salmon: Place 4 salmon fillets, skin-side down, on a baking sheet lined with parchment paper. Pat the filets dry with a paper towel to ensure they cook evenly.

3. Season: Drizzle the salmon with olive oil, then sprinkle with salt, black pepper, and minced garlic. Arrange a few thin lemon slices on each fillet and scatter fresh dill sprigs on top for an aromatic touch.

4. Bake: Bake for 12-15 minutes, depending on the thickness of the fillets, until the salmon is flaky and opaque in the center.

5. Serve: Transfer the filets to plates and serve with a squeeze of fresh lemon juice. Pair with roasted vegetables, quinoa, or a side salad for a complete meal.

This dish is perfect for those looking for a healthy, quick dinner without sacrificing taste. The combination of lemon and dill complements the salmon beautifully, while the simple preparation lets the fish's natural flavor shine. With minimal cleanup and wholesome ingredients, baked salmon with lemon and dill is a fantastic option for both busy weeknights and special occasions.

44

2• Herbed Cod with Roasted Tomatoes

Herbed cod with roasted tomatoes is a delicate and flavorful dish that highlights the lightness of cod and the rich, caramelized taste of oven-roasted tomatoes. Cod, a lean fish with a mild flavor, works beautifully with aromatic herbs and a burst of acidity from the tomatoes. This dish is both nutritious and satisfying, providing a good dose of protein along with antioxidants from the tomato's

How to Prepare:

1. Preheat the Oven: Set the oven to 400°F (200°C).

2. Prepare the Tomatoes: Halve 2 cups of cherry or grape tomatoes and place them on a baking sheet. Drizzle with olive oil, sprinkle with salt and pepper, and toss in a few cloves of smashed garlic. Roast for 20–25 minutes until soft and slightly charred.

3. Season the Cod: While the tomatoes roast, season 4 cod fillets with olive oil, salt, pepper, and a mix of fresh herbs—such as parsley, thyme, and oregano. Optionally, add a bit of lemon zest for an extra layer of brightness.

4. Bake the Cod: Arrange the cod fillets on a separate baking sheet or in a baking dish. Bake for 12–15 minutes or until the fish is opaque and flakes easily with a fork.

5. Combine and Serve: Spoon the roasted tomatoes over the baked cod and drizzle with the juices from the tomatoes. Garnish with additional herbs and a squeeze of lemon. Serve with a side of roasted vegetables, quinoa, or a light salad.

This dish offers a beautiful combination of simplicity and depth. The cod remains tender and flaky, while the roasted tomatoes provide sweetness and a subtle tang that enhances the flavor of the fish. With its clean ingredients and straightforward preparation, herbed cod with roasted tomatoes is perfect for a wholesome, weeknight meal or a light yet refined dinner.

- **3• Chicken Stir-Fry with Broccoli**

Chicken stir-fry with broccoli is a vibrant, wholesome dish that brings together tender chicken, crisp broccoli, and a flavorful sauce. It's a popular choice for a quick, balanced meal, rich in protein, fiber, vitamins, and essential minerals. The simplicity of stir-frying helps retain the vegetables' nutrients and ensures the chicken remains juicy and flavorful.

How to Prepare:

1. Prep the Ingredients: Slice 1 lb of chicken breast into thin strips for faster cooking. Cut 2-3 cups of broccoli into bite-sized florets. Mince 3 garlic cloves and slice a small onion for added flavor.

2. Make the Sauce: In a bowl, whisk together ¼ cup of soy sauce (or tamari for gluten-free), 2 tablespoons of honey, 1 tablespoon of sesame oil, 1 tablespoon of rice vinegar, and 1 teaspoon of cornstarch. This sauce provides the perfect balance of sweet, savory, and umami flavors.

3. Cook the Chicken: Heat a tablespoon of oil in a large skillet or wok over medium-high heat. Add the chicken strips and stir-fry for 5-6 minutes, until lightly browned and cooked through. Transfer to a plate and set aside.

- **4. Sauté the Vegetables**: In the same pan, add a bit more oil if needed. Stir-fry the broccoli, garlic, and onions for 3-4 minutes until the vegetables are tender-crisp but still vibrant in color.

5. Combine and Toss: Return the chicken to the pan. Pour in the prepared sauce and stir everything together until the sauce thickens and coats the ingredients evenly. Cook for an additional 1-2 minutes to ensure the flavors meld.

6. Serve: Serve the stir-fry over steamed rice, quinoa, or cauliflower rice. Garnish with sesame seeds or green onions for extra flavor

This dish is both adaptable and nutritious, with the option to add other vegetables like bell peppers, snap peas, or carrots. Chicken stir-fry with broccoli offers a perfect balance of textures and flavors, making it ideal for busy weeknights. It's a great way to enjoy a hearty yet healthy meal without compromising on taste or convenience.

4• Grilled Tuna Salad with Avocado

Grilled tuna salad with avocado offers a refreshing, nutrient-dense meal that balances lean protein with healthy fats. The combination of seared tuna and creamy avocado creates a satisfying dish ideal for lunch or dinner. Tuna, packed with omega-3 fatty acids, supports heart health, while avocado provides essential fats and fiber, making this salad both flavorful and nourishing.

How to Prepare:

1. Grill the Tuna: Season fresh tuna steaks with olive oil, salt, pepper, and a pinch of paprika or garlic powder. Heat a grill or grill pan to high and sear the tuna for 2-3 minutes on each side, leaving the center rare or cooked to your preference. Set aside to rest before slicing.

2. Prepare the Salad Base: In a large bowl, combine mixed greens or arugula with cherry tomatoes, thinly sliced red onions, and cucumber. For additional texture, add a handful of sunflower seeds or slivered almonds.

3. Slice the Avocado: Halve, pit, and scoop out the flesh of one ripe avocado. Slice it thinly or cube it for easy mixing with the greens.

4. Make the Dressing: Whisk together 3 tablespoons of olive oil, the juice of 1 lemon, 1 teaspoon of Dijon mustard, salt, and pepper. Optional: Add a pinch of red pepper flakes for a subtle kick.

5. Assemble the Salad: Arrange the grilled tuna slices on top of the salad. Add the avocado slices and drizzle with the dressing.

6. Serve: Garnish with fresh herbs like parsley or chives, and enjoy with a piece of whole-grain bread or quinoa on the side.

This salad is light yet hearty, offering a great balance of proteins, healthy fats, and fresh vegetables. It's ideal for those seeking a nutritious, quick-to-make meal with gourmet appeal. The charred tuna contrasts beautifully with the creamy avocado and crisp vegetables, making every bite a delightful mix of flavors and textures.

5• Turmeric Chicken with Quinoa

Turmeric chicken with quinoa is a vibrant, nourishing dish that combines the anti-inflammatory benefits of turmeric with the wholesome, nutty flavor of quinoa. This meal is rich in lean protein, complex carbohydrates, and essential nutrients, making it an excellent option for both lunch and dinner. The earthy warmth of turmeric pairs beautifully with tender chicken, while quinoa adds texture and depth.

How to Prepare:

1. Marinate the Chicken: In a bowl, mix 2 teaspoons of ground turmeric, 1 teaspoon cumin, minced garlic, salt, pepper, and 2 tablespoons olive oil. Coat the chicken breasts or thighs evenly in the marinade and let them sit for at least 30 minutes to absorb the flavors.

2. Cook the Quinoa: Rinse 1 cup of quinoa under cold water. In a saucepan, combine the quinoa with 2 cups of water or broth, bring to a boil, reduce the heat, and simmer for 15-20 minutes until the quinoa is fluffy and the liquid is absorbed. Fluff with a fork and season lightly with salt.

3. Sear the Chicken: Heat a skillet over medium heat and cook the marinated chicken for 5-7 minutes on each side until golden brown and cooked through. Let the chicken rest for a few minutes before slicing.

4. Assemble the Dish: Serve the chicken over a bed of quinoa. For added flavor and color, top with fresh herbs like cilantro or parsley, and drizzle with lemon juice. Optionally, add roasted vegetables or sautéed greens for a complete meal.

This dish is simple yet packed with flavor and nutritional value. The turmeric lends a golden hue and subtle spice, while quinoa offers a high-protein, gluten-free base. It's a versatile recipe that can be adapted to suit various diets—substitute tofu or chickpeas for a plant-based option or swap the quinoa with brown rice. The bright flavors and wholesome ingredients make this dish both enjoyable and energizing.

F• Vegetables & Sides

1• Roasted Brussels Sprouts with Balsamic Glaze

Roasted Brussels sprouts with balsamic glaze is a simple yet flavorful side dish that combines crispy textures with a perfect balance of sweetness and tang. Brussels sprouts are packed with fiber, vitamins, and antioxidants, and roasting enhances their natural sweetness while adding a slightly caramelized edge.

How to Prepare:

1. Preheat the Oven: Set the oven to 400°F (200°C).

2. Prepare the Sprouts: Trim the ends and halve the Brussels sprouts. Toss them with olive oil, salt, and black pepper.

3. Roast: Arrange the sprouts cut-side down on a baking sheet and roast for 20–25 minutes, flipping halfway through for even browning.

4. Make the Balsamic Glaze: Simmer ½ cup of balsamic vinegar over medium heat until it reduces by half and thickens to a syrup-like consistency. Add a teaspoon of honey or maple syrup if you want extra sweetness.

5. Serve: Drizzle the glaze over the roasted sprouts and garnish with toasted nuts, dried cranberries, or parmesan for added texture and flavor.

This dish offers a great mix of crispy, savory, and tangy elements. The balsamic glaze adds a touch of complexity, balancing the sprouts' earthy flavor with a slightly sweet note. It works well as a side to roasted meats or as part of a plant-based meal, bringing both nutrition and taste to the table.

2• Steamed Asparagus with Olive Oil

Steamed asparagus with olive oil is a simple, nutritious side dish that highlights the vegetable's natural flavor and vibrant color. Asparagus is rich in vitamins A, C, and K, along with folate and antioxidants. Steaming preserves its delicate texture and nutrients while ensuring it doesn't become soggy.

How to Prepare:

1. Trim the Asparagus: Snap or cut off the woody ends from the stalks.

2. Steam: Place the asparagus in a steamer basket over boiling water. Cover and steam for 4–5 minutes until tender but still crisp.

3. Finish with Olive Oil: Transfer the asparagus to a serving dish and drizzle with high-quality extra virgin olive oil.

4. Optional Garnishes: Season with salt and pepper. Add a squeeze of lemon, shaved parmesan, or toasted almonds for added flavor.

This dish is elegant in its simplicity. The olive oil enhances the asparagus's mild, grassy notes without overpowering it. It pairs wonderfully with grilled meats, fish, or plant-based mains and is ideal for a light, healthy accompaniment.

3• Sweet Potato Fries

Sweet potato fries are a healthier twist on classic fries, offering a blend of natural sweetness and savory flavors. Packed with fiber, vitamins A and C, and antioxidants, sweet potatoes provide essential nutrients while satisfying cravings. Baking them instead of frying keeps them light, while still delivering crisp edges and soft interiors.

How to Prepare:

1. Preheat the Oven: Set to 425°F (220°C).

2. Slice the Potatoes: Cut sweet potatoes into evenly sized sticks to ensure consistent cooking.

3. Season: Toss the fries with olive oil, salt, and optional spices like paprika, garlic powder, or cumin.

4. Bake: Spread them in a single layer on a baking sheet. Bake for 25–30 minutes, flipping halfway through for even browning.

5. Serve: Enjoy them hot, paired with dips like garlic aioli, guacamole, or a tangy yogurt sauce.

Sweet potato fries are a great side dish for burgers, sandwiches, or wraps, but they can also stand alone as a tasty snack. Their natural sweetness pairs well with a variety of seasonings, making them highly versatile. For added crispness, you can lightly coat the fries with corn
starch before baking.

4• Cauliflower Rice Pilaf
Cauliflower Rice Pilaf

Cauliflower rice pilaf is a light, flavorful dish that serves as a low-carb alternative to traditional grain-based pilafs. Made from finely chopped cauliflower florets, this dish offers a satisfying texture and subtle taste, while also being rich in vitamins C and K, antioxidants, and fiber. It's perfect as a side or base for other proteins, and its mild flavor makes it highly versatile.

How to Prepare:

1. Prepare the Cauliflower: Break a head of cauliflower into florets and pulse in a food processor until it resembles rice.

2. Sauté Aromatics: Heat olive oil in a large skillet over medium heat. Sauté diced onions and minced garlic until fragrant. Optionally, add spices like cumin or turmeric for an extra layer of flavor.

3. Cook the Cauliflower: Add the cauliflower rice to the skillet and stir for 5–7 minutes until it softens. Avoid overcooking to maintain some texture.

4. Add Vegetables and Herbs: Toss in chopped bell peppers, peas, or spinach for added nutrients. Finish with fresh herbs such as parsley or cilantro.

5. Season and Serve: Adjust with salt, pepper, and a squeeze of lemon for brightness.

This dish works well as a side for grilled meats, roasted vegetables, or even fish. It can be customized with nuts, seeds, or dried fruit to add both texture and flavor. The quick preparation makes cauliflower rice pilaf a great option for weeknight dinners, while its nutrient profile aligns with many diets, including paleo,
keto, and gluten-free.

5• Sautéed Spinach with Garlic

Sautéed spinach with garlic is a simple, nutrient-rich side dish that elevates the natural flavors of spinach with aromatic garlic. Spinach is packed with iron, calcium, and vitamins A and C, while garlic brings anti-inflammatory benefits and a savory punch. This dish is quick to prepare and pairs well with almost any main course.

How to Prepare:

1. Heat the Oil: Warm 1–2 tablespoons of olive oil in a large skillet over medium heat.

2. Add Garlic: Sauté thinly sliced garlic for 30 seconds until fragrant but not browned.

3. Add the Spinach: Toss in fresh spinach leaves, stirring occasionally until just wilted (2–3 minutes). Work in batches if needed.

4. Season: Sprinkle with salt, pepper, and a pinch of red pepper flakes for heat, if desired.

5. Serve: Drizzle with lemon juice for brightness or top with grated Parmesan for added richness.

This dish offers vibrant color and delicate flavor without overpowering the meal. Its simplicity allows for endless variations—you can add pine nuts, raisins, or feta for more complexity. It pairs well with grilled meats, roasted fish, or legumes, making it a go-to side for various dietary preferences.

G• Desserts & Treats

1• Chia Seed Pudding with Mango

Chia seed pudding with mango is a refreshing and nutritious treat that makes a great breakfast, snack, or dessert. Chia seeds are rich in omega-3 fatty acids, fiber, and protein, while mango adds natural sweetness and a tropical flair. The pudding has a creamy texture, thanks to the gelatinous quality of soaked chia seeds, which absorb liquid and swell over time.

How to Prepare:

1. Combine Ingredients: In a bowl or jar, mix 3 tablespoons of chia seeds with 1 cup of plant-based milk (like almond or coconut milk). Stir in a teaspoon of maple syrup or honey for sweetness, if desired.

2. Let it Set: Cover and refrigerate for at least 4 hours or overnight. Stir the mixture once after 10–15 minutes to prevent clumping.

3. Prepare the Mango: Peel and dice a ripe mango, or blend it into a puree if you prefer a smoother topping.

4. Assemble: Layer the mango chunks or puree over the chilled chia pudding. Optional toppings include shredded coconut, nuts, or fresh mint for extra flavor and texture.

This pudding is easy to customize, making it a versatile option for different dietary needs. You can swap mango with other fruits like berries or pineapple and experiment with flavored milks or spices such as cinnamon. It offers a satisfying balance of creamy, fruity, and nutrient-dense elements, making it an excellent choice for those seeking a wholesome, make-ahead meal or snack

2• Dark Chocolate Almond Bark

Dark chocolate almond bark is an indulgent yet healthy snack that combines the richness of dark chocolate with the crunch of roasted almonds. It's a simple, elegant treat perfect for snacking, gifting, or serving as a dessert. Rich in antioxidants from the dark chocolate and healthy fats from the almonds, this bark provides both flavor and nutritional benefits.

How to Prepare:

1. Melt the Chocolate: Use a double boiler or microwave in short intervals to melt 8–10 ounces of dark chocolate (70% cocoa or higher). Stir until smooth.

2. Prepare the Almonds: Toast 1 cup of almonds in the oven or on the stovetop for a few minutes to enhance their flavor. Let them cool.

3. Combine: Mix the almonds into the melted chocolate, ensuring they are well coated. You can also add a pinch of sea salt or sprinkle with dried fruit for added texture.

4. Spread and Set: Pour the mixture onto a parchment-lined baking sheet and spread it evenly. Refrigerate for 30–40 minutes until firm.

5. Break into Pieces: Once hardened, break the bark into bite-sized chunks. Store in an airtight container at room temperature or in the fridge.

This bark is highly customizable—swap almonds for hazelnuts, add seeds, or incorporate spices like cinnamon for variation. It strikes a great balance between satisfying a sweet tooth and supporting a healthy diet.

3• Baked Apples with Cinnamon

Baked apples with cinnamon are a cozy, wholesome dessert that offers a perfect blend of natural sweetness and warm spice. Apples provide fiber and antioxidants, while cinnamon enhances the dish with its aromatic, anti-inflammatory properties. This dessert is light yet satisfying, making it ideal for those looking to enjoy a treat without added guilt.

How to Prepare:

1. Preheat the Oven: Set to 375°F (190°C).

2. Core the Apples: Remove the cores of 4 apples, leaving the bottom intact to hold the filling.

3. Prepare the Filling: Mix 2 tablespoons of oats, 1 tablespoon of maple syrup or honey, a dash of cinnamon, and a handful of chopped nuts or raisins.

4. Stuff the Apples: Spoon the filling into the hollowed cores.

5. Bake: Place the apples in a baking dish and add a little water to the bottom of the dish. Cover with foil and bake for 25–30 minutes until tender.

6. Serve: Drizzle with more honey or maple syrup and enjoy as is or with a dollop of yogurt or whipped cream.

This dish is both rustic and refined, highlighting the apple's natural flavor while infusing it with warmth from the cinnamon. You can adjust the filling to your liking, adding different nuts, seeds, or spices for variety. Baked apples are perfect for cool evenings and pair wonderfully with tea or coffee, offering a healthier alternative to traditional desserts.

4• Coconut Macaroons

Coconut macaroons are sweet, chewy treats with a crisp exterior and soft, flavorful interior. Made primarily from shredded coconut, these cookies are naturally gluten-free and simple to prepare. They make a delightful dessert or snack, often enjoyed plain or dipped in chocolate for an extra indulgence.

How to Prepare:

1. Preheat the Oven: Set to 350°F (175°C).

2. Mix Ingredients: In a bowl, combine 2 ½ cups of shredded coconut, ½ cup of sweetened condensed milk, and 1 teaspoon of vanilla extract.

3. Whisk Egg Whites: Beat two egg whites with a pinch of salt until stiff peaks form. Gently fold them into the coconut mixture.

4. Shape and Bake: Drop spoonfuls of the batter onto a parchment-lined baking sheet. Bake for 15–20 minutes or until the tops are golden brown.

5. Cool and Serve: Let them cool before serving. Optional: Dip the bottoms in melted chocolate once cooled.

These macaroons are perfect for holidays, afternoon tea, or anytime you crave a bite-sized treat. With minimal ingredients, they're easy to customize—add citrus zest for brightness, or drizzle with dark chocolate for a more decadent version. Their dense, chewy texture makes them satisfying without b eing overly heavy.

5• Avocado Chocolate Mousse

Avocado chocolate mousse is a creamy, nutrient-packed dessert that offers a healthier twist on traditional mousse. Avocados bring richness and heart-healthy fats, while dark cocoa powder adds depth without the need for heavy cream. Naturally dairy-free and refined-sugar optional, it's perfect for those seeking a decadent treat with a nutritional boost.

How to Prepare:

1. Blend Ingredients: Combine 2 ripe avocados, ¼ cup cocoa powder, ¼ cup maple syrup or honey, 1 teaspoon vanilla extract, and a pinch of sea salt in a blender.

2. Adjust Consistency: Add a few tablespoons of almond or oat milk to achieve the desired texture. Blend until smooth and creamy.

3. Chill: Refrigerate for 30 minutes to enhance the flavors and texture.

4. Serve: Divide into individual bowls and top with fresh berries, chopped nuts, or shredded coconut.

This mousse is rich and indulgent without being overly heavy, making it an ideal dessert for those following vegan or gluten-free diets. The avocado flavor is subtle, allowing the chocolate to shine through. You can also experiment with spices like cinnamon or cayenne to add complexity. Enjoy it guilt-free as a post-dinner dessert or an after
noon indulgence.

PART IV: WEEK-BY-WEEK MEAL PLANS & SHOPPING LISTS

Week-By-Week Meal Plans & Shopping Lists

This section provides a practical, step-by-step guide for following an anti-inflammatory diet across several weeks. Each week includes carefully structured meal plans that focus on variety, balance, and ease of preparation. The goal is to help you stay on track with minimal stress, ensuring meals are nutritious while catering to different dietary needs.

How It Works

1. Weekly Overview: Each week outlines a set of breakfasts, lunches, dinners, and snacks. Meals are designed to minimize inflammation and rotate key ingredients like leafy greens, healthy fats, whole grains, and lean proteins.

2. Shopping Lists: Each week is accompanied by a complete shopping list, broken down by category (produce, pantry items, proteins, etc.). These lists reduce time spent at the store and ensure you have everything you need for the week.

3. Meal Prep Tips: Suggestions for batch cooking and make-ahead meals are provided to streamline the process. For example, prepping quinoa or roasting vegetables on Sunday allows for easy assembly of meals throughout the week.

Sample Weekly Plan Outline

- **Breakfasts:** Smoothies, oatmeal variations, chia puddings

- **Lunches**: Salads with hearty grains, soups, or protein bowls

- **Dinners**: Lean proteins like salmon, paired with vegetables and whole grains

- **Snacks:** Hummus with veggies, nuts, or roasted chickpeas

Each plan ensures meals are diverse and aligned with the diet's anti-inflammatory principles, preventing boredom while maintaining balance. You can adjust portions or ingredients to suit personal preferences or dietary restrictions. Flexibility is key—alternatives are offered for gluten-free, vegan, and pescatarian diets, ensuring the plans fit seamlessly into your lifestyle.

With clear shopping lists and meal-prep strategies, this section takes the guesswork out of healthy eating, making it easier to stay consistent and build long-term habits.

Week 2: Adding Variety and New Flavors

In Week 2, the focus shifts toward expanding your palate with diverse ingredients and bold flavors, ensuring the anti-inflammatory diet remains enjoyable and sustainable. Introducing new spices, herbs, and culturally inspired dishes not only keeps meals exciting but also boosts the health benefits by incorporating a broader range of antioxidants and nutrients.

Key Strategies for Week 2

1. Experiment with Global Cuisines:
Explore flavors from Mediterranean, Thai, or Middle Eastern cuisines. Incorporate spices like turmeric, cumin, ginger, and za'atar to elevate meals. Examples include roasted vegetables with harissa or quinoa bowls with tahini dressing.

2. Include New Vegetables and Grains:
Try incorporating nutrient-dense options such as fennel, bok choy, millet, or wild rice to add texture and diversity. These swaps not only boost the nutrient profile but prevent food fatigue.

3. Use Fresh Herbs Generously:
Add basil, cilantro, mint, and parsley to salads, soups, and entrees. Fresh herbs brighten dishes and offer anti-inflammatory compounds that support digestion and immunity.

4. Embrace Fermented Foods:
Add probiotic-rich foods like sauerkraut, kimchi, and miso to promote gut health, which is crucial for managing inflammation. These foods pair well with salads, stir-fries, or grain bowls.

5. Incorporate Healthy Flavor Enhancers:
Use citrus zest, infused oils, or toasted seeds to enhance flavor naturally. For example, lemon zest can bring brightness to grilled fish, while toasted sesame seeds add depth to vegetable stir-fries.

Sample Dishes for Week 2

• **Breakfast:** Smoothie bowl with mango, mint, and chia seeds

• **Lunch:** Quinoa salad with roasted vegetables, parsley, and a lemon-tahini dressing

• **Dinner:** Coconut curry with chickpeas and basmati rice

• **Snacks:** Roasted almonds with smoked paprika or hummus with sliced cucumber

This week emphasizes the importance of variety in both ingredients and techniques. It encourages home cooks to step out of their comfort zones by trying new ingredients and exploring culinary traditions from around the world. These new flavors and textures ensure that healthy eating feels like an adventure rather than a chore.

1. **Week 3: Seasonal and Budget-Friendly Ideas**

Week 3 focuses on making the anti-inflammatory diet accessible and economical by using seasonal produce and budget-friendly ingredients. This approach not only supports local farmers but also enhances the flavor and nutritional quality of your meals. By emphasizing fresh, in-season items, you can create vibrant dishes that are both satisfying and easy on the wallet.

Key Strategies for Week 3

1. Embrace Seasonal Produce:
Take advantage of fruits and vegetables that are currently in season. For instance, in the summer, you might use tomatoes, zucchini, and berries, while autumn brings squash, apples, and leafy greens. Seasonal ingredients often taste better and are more affordable.

2. Plan Around Sales:
Check local grocery store flyers and farmers' markets for sales on fresh produce and pantry staples. Planning meals around these discounts can si.gnificantly reduce grocery costs. For example, if sweet potatoes are on sale, consider incorporating them into various meals throughout the week.

3 Cook in Batches:
Prepare larger portions of recipes that can be enjoyed over several days or frozen for later. Dishes like soups, stews, and casseroles can be made in advance, providing quick and easy meals throughout the week.

1. **4. Utilize Whole Grains:** Incorporate budget-friendly grains like brown rice, barley, or oats. These grains are not only affordable but also filling and nutritious. They can serve as the base for salads, bowls, or as sides.

5. Get Creative with Leftovers:
Transform leftovers into new meals. For example, roasted vegetables can become a frittata or a grain bowl. This not only reduces food waste but also keeps meals interesting.

Sample Dishes for Week 3

- **Breakfast:** Overnight oats topped with seasonal fruit and a sprinkle of cinnamon
- Lunch: Lentil salad with chopped seasonal vegetables and a vinaigrette
- **Dinner:** Stuffed bell peppers with quinoa, black beans, and diced tomatoes
- **Snacks:** Sliced apples with almond butter or homemade popcorn seasoned with herbs

By focusing on seasonal produce and budget-friendly ingredients, this week emphasizes the importance of eating well without overspending. You'll discover that nutritious meals can be both affordable and delicious, making healthy eating an achievable goal for everyone. This approach not only fosters creativity in the kitchen but also promotes a more sustainable way of eating.

Week 4: Advanced Batch Cooking Techniques

In the fourth week, the focus shifts to mastering advanced batch cooking techniques that can streamline meal preparation and make healthy eating even more convenient. By employing these methods, you can optimize your time in the kitchen, reduce food waste, and ensure that your meals are both nutritious and satisfying.

Key Techniques for Effective Batch Cooking

1. Meal Prepping Essentials:
Begin by designating a specific day for meal prepping each week. This could be a Sunday or any day that suits your schedule. During this time, prepare multiple meals that can be consumed throughout the week. This not only saves time but also alleviates the stress of daily cooking.

2. Investing in Quality Storage Containers:
Choose airtight containers that are stackable and easy to label. Glass containers are excellent for reheating in the oven or microwave, while BPA-free plastic options can be convenient for on-the-go meals. Proper storage helps maintain freshness and flavor while minimizing waste.

3. Using Slow Cookers and Pressure Cookers:
Take advantage of slow cookers or pressure cookers like the Instant Pot. These appliances allow for hands-off cooking, making it easy to prepare large batches of soups, stews, and grains. For instance, a big pot of chili can be made in a few hours and portioned for the week ahead.

4. Creating Base Components:
Cook staple ingredients in bulk, such as grains (quinoa, brown rice), legumes (beans, lentils), and proteins (chicken, tofu). These base components can serve as the foundation for various meals, making it easy to mix and match throughout the week. For example, grilled chicken can be added to salads, wraps, or grain bowls.

5. Maximizing Flavor with Seasoning:
When batch cooking, experiment with different herbs and spices to enhance the flavor of your dishes. Preparing marinated proteins or seasoned vegetables ahead of time can transform basic ingredients into delicious meals. Consider using marinades for proteins that can be refrigerated overnight for better flavor absorption.

6. Freezer-Friendly Options:
Not all meals can be made in one sitting, so learn which dishes freeze well. Soups, casseroles, and baked goods are typically great options. Portion these meals into individual servings before freezing to simplify reheating later on. Label them with dates and ingredients for easy identification.

7. Repurposing Leftovers Creatively:
Transforming leftovers into new meals can keep your menu exciting. For example, roasted vegetables from one night can be incorporated into a breakfast frittata or served on top of a grain bowl. This approach minimizes waste and ensures that you're making the most of your cooking efforts.

Sample Dishes for Week 4

- Breakfast: Overnight oats prepared with seasonal fruits and nuts, stored in grab-and-go containers.
- Lunch: A hearty vegetable and lentil soup made in bulk and portioned out for easy lunches throughout the week.
- Dinner: Stuffed bell peppers filled with a mixture of quinoa, black beans, and spices, ready to bake and serve.
- Snacks: Energy balls made from oats, nut butter, and seeds, prepped in advance for quick snacking.

By implementing these advanced batch cooking techniques, you'll not only save time and effort but also cultivate a more organized and enjoyable approach to your anti-inflammatory diet. This week emphasizes the power of preparation, allowing you to eat well while managing a busy lifestyle.

60

Part V: Troubleshooting and Motivation

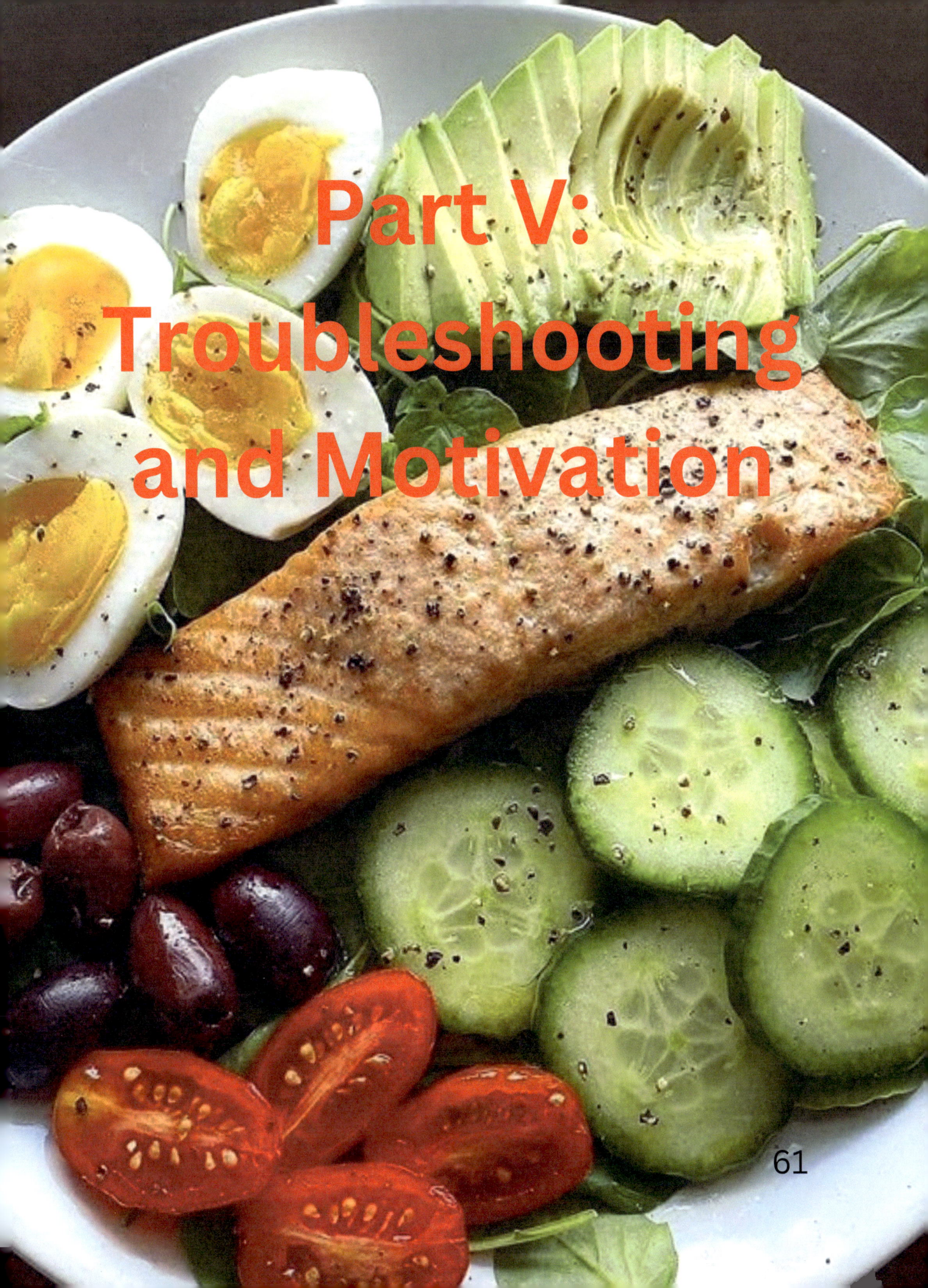

1.1 • Handling Cravings and Cheat Days

Navigating cravings and cheat days is an essential aspect of maintaining an anti-inflammatory diet without feeling deprived. Understanding how to manage these moments can lead to a more sustainable and enjoyable eating experience.

Understanding Cravings

1. Identify Triggers:
Recognizing what prompts your cravings is the first step in managing them. Stress, boredom, or specific environmental cues can lead to the desire for certain foods. By being aware of these triggers, you can develop strategies to counteract them.

2. Opt for Healthy Alternatives:
When cravings strike, seek out healthier options that satisfy the same urge. For instance, if you crave something sweet, consider reaching for fruit or a yogurt parfait instead of processed snacks. This way, you indulge without straying from your dietary goals.

3. Stay Hydrated:
Sometimes, cravings can be mistaken for thirst. Keeping yourself well-hydrated throughout the day may help mitigate unwanted cravings. Aim for at least eight glasses of water daily and consider herbal teas as a comforting option.

4. Mindful Eating:
Practicing mindfulness can enhance your relationship with food. Take time to savor your meals, paying attention to flavors and textures. This conscious approach not only improves satisfaction but also reduces the likelihood of impulsive eating.

5. Balanced Nutrition:
Ensuring your meals are balanced with adequate protein, healthy fats, and fiber can keep you feeling full longer. When your body receives the nutrients it needs, you may find that cravings become less frequent.

Cheat Days: A Balanced Approach

1. Redefining Cheat Days:
Rather than viewing cheat days as a break from a diet, consider them an opportunity to enjoy your favorite foods in moderation. This mindset shift can reduce feelings of guilt and help you maintain a healthy relationship with food.

2. Plan Ahead:
If you know you'll be indulging in certain foods, plan for it. Designate a specific day for your cheat meals, and prepare in advance. This preparation can help you avoid overindulging and maintain control.

3. Portion Control:
On cheat days, practice portion control. Enjoying a small piece of cake or a few bites of pizza can be satisfying without leading to excessive calorie consumption. The goal is to relish the experience without derailing your overall diet.

4. Focus on Quality:
Choose high-quality foods that you truly enjoy for your cheat meals. Instead of eating mindlessly, select items that are worth the indulgence, whether that's a rich dessert or a favorite savory dish.

5. Reassess After Indulging:
After a cheat day, take time to reflect on how you feel both physically and emotionally. Recognizing how your body reacts to certain foods can help inform future choices, allowing you to strike a balance between enjoyment and health.

By understanding cravings and approaching cheat days thoughtfully, you can create a sustainable anti-inflammatory eating pattern. This balanced approach fosters a healthier relationship with food, helping you stay committed to your dietary goals while still allowing for occasional indulgences.

2. Adapting the Diet for Families

Incorporating an anti-inflammatory diet into family life can seem daunting, but with thoughtful adjustments, it's entirely manageable. The goal is to foster healthy habits for everyone while making meals enjoyable and accessible.

Getting the Family Onboard

1. Education through Involvement:
Explain the benefits of the diet to family members, focusing on how it supports energy, immunity, and overall health. Involve children in meal planning, grocery shopping, or cooking to make the transition smoother.

2. Gradual Changes Over Time:
Introduce new foods slowly. Swap out refined grains with whole grains like quinoa or oats, and replace sugary drinks with naturally flavored water. Gradual modifications ensure less resistance and allow everyone to adjust.

3. Emphasize Familiarity with a Twist:
Keep family favorites on the menu but with a healthier spin. For example, replace white pasta with zucchini noodles or incorporate more vegetables into tacos. This approach retains comfort while promoting wellness.

Meal Planning for Multiple Preferences

1. Flexible Recipes:
Prepare meals that allow customization, like grain bowls or build-your-own tacos. These options accommodate different preferences without requiring separate meals for each person.

2. Batch Cooking for Busy Days:
Cook in bulk to save time. Prepare large portions of soups, roasted vegetables, or grilled proteins that can be mixed and matched throughout the week.

3. Kid-Friendly Snacks:
1. Offer nutritious options like hummus with veggie sticks, trail mix, or fruit yogurt parfaits to replace less healthy snacks. Making snacks visually appealing encourages children to try new foods.

Handling Picky Eaters

1. Exposure Without Pressure:
Research shows that repeated exposure to new foods increases acceptance. Encourage kids to try new ingredients, but avoid forcing them.

2. Modeling Behavior:
Children learn eating habits by observing adults. When they see parents enjoying healthy meals, they're more likely to follow suit.

3. Incorporating Fun:
Turn meal preparation into a family activity. Use fun names for healthy foods, like "power greens," or arrange food in creative shapes to engage younger children.

Balancing Indulgence and Health

It's important to allow occasional treats to avoid making the diet feel restrictive. Designate days for family indulgences with homemade versions of favorite foods, like whole-wheat pizzas or fruit-based desserts. Teaching balance ensures that children develop a positive, sustainable relationship with food.

Adapting an anti-inflammatory diet for families requires flexibility, patience, and creativity. By making small changes and involving everyone in the process, the diet becomes less about restriction and more about fostering health in a way that fits the family's lifestyle.

3• Common Pitfalls to Avoid

When following an anti-inflammatory diet, people often encounter several challenges. Knowing these common pitfalls can help you stay on track and achieve lasting results without unnecessary setbacks.

1. Over-Restricting Foods

Trying to eliminate too many foods at once can make the diet feel overwhelming and unsustainable. While it's important to avoid processed items, over-restriction can lead to frustration and cravings. Focus on what you can add—like more fruits, vegetables, and healthy fats—rather than just eliminating foods.

2. Lack of Planning

Failing to plan meals and snacks can lead to last-minute decisions, increasing the likelihood of unhealthy choices. Regular meal planning, batch cooking, and grocery shopping help you stay organized and prevent impulsive eating.

3. Ignoring Portion Control

Even healthy foods, when consumed in excess, can lead to weight gain and disrupt progress. Pay attention to portion sizes, especially with calorie-dense ingredients like nuts, oils, and avocados. Balance meals by including proteins, fiber, and healthy fats.

4. Relying Too Heavily on Processed "Healthy" Foods

Packaged foods labeled as "organic," "gluten-free," or "plant-based" are not always nutritious. Many still contain added sugars, sodium, and unhealthy fats. Prioritize whole, unprocessed ingredients and check labels carefully to avoid hidden additives.

5. Skipping Meals or Under-Eating

Skipping meals can lead to energy crashes, cravings, and overeating later in the day. Consistent, well-balanced meals keep blood sugar levels stable and support energy levels throughout the day.

6. Failing to Stay Hydrated

Dehydration is a common issue that can be mistaken for hunger. Drinking water regularly throughout the day is essential for optimal digestion and overall health. Incorporate herbal teas or infused water to make hydration more appealing.

7. Not Listening to Your Body

Every person's needs are different, and what works for one may not suit another. Pay attention to how your body responds to certain foods, and adjust accordingly. Experiment with different ingredients and meal timings to find what best supports your well-being.

8. Neglecting Social Situations

Navigating social gatherings while following a specific diet can be challenging. Plan ahead by eating beforehand or bringing a dish to share. Communicate your dietary preferences with hosts to ensure you have suitable options.

9. Giving Up After a Slip

Experiencing setbacks is part of the process. If you indulge in a treat or miss a few healthy meals, don't let it derail your efforts. View slip-ups as learning opportunities and refocus without guilt.

Avoiding these common mistakes can make your journey with an anti-inflammatory diet smoother and more sustainable. Embrace flexibility, stay mindful of your body's needs, and celebrate progress rather than perfection.

4• Staying Motivated and Tracking Progress

Maintaining motivation while following an anti-inflammatory diet is essential for long-term success. It requires intentional strategies to overcome challenges and consistently monitor improvements without feeling overwhelmed.

1. Set Realistic and Specific Goals

Instead of vague objectives like "eat healthier," define achievable targets, such as cooking at home four nights a week or incorporating one anti-inflammatory meal per day. Break your larger goals into smaller, actionable steps to build momentum.

2. Track Progress Beyond Weight Loss

While weight is often a focus, tracking non-scale victories, such as improved energy, clearer skin, or better digestion, provides more meaningful motivation. Keep a journal of how you feel physically and emotionally as you incorporate new foods.

3. Use Habit-Tracking Tools

Apps, journals, or habit trackers are excellent for staying organized. Log meals, symptoms, or cravings to identify trends. This will help you adjust the diet as needed while reinforcing positive habits through visual progress.

4. Celebrate Small Wins

Every positive change is worth celebrating—whether it's trying a new recipe, successfully meal prepping for the week, or choosing a healthy snack over processed options. Acknowledging these moments boosts morale and builds confidence.

5. Create a Support Network

Engage with friends, family, or online communities for encouragement and accountability. Sharing experiences makes the process more enjoyable, and having someone to check in with helps you stay on track.

6. Adapt as Needed

Recognize that life is unpredictable. If you encounter obstacles, adjust your plan without guilt. Flexibility ensures that temporary setbacks don't derail your progress.

7. Revisit Your "Why"

When motivation wanes, remind yourself why you started. Whether your goal is to reduce chronic inflammation, boost energy, or prevent disease, keeping that purpose in mind will help you push through challenges.

8. Make It Enjoyable

Experiment with recipes, try new ingredients, and treat cooking as an enjoyable activity rather than a chore. Finding joy in the process keeps you engaged and motivated.

Staying motivated requires a blend of planning, reflection, and celebrating progress. By tracking both tangible and intangible improvements, adjusting your approach, and surrounding yourself with support, you'll be better equipped to stay consistent on your anti-inflammatory journey.

5• Eating Out While Staying on Track

Dining out can feel tricky when following an anti-inflammatory diet, but with thoughtful planning, you can enjoy meals out without compromising your goals. Here are strategies to help you navigate restaurant menus while staying aligned with your dietary needs.

1. Research Menus Ahead of Time

Many restaurants post their menus online, allowing you to review options before arriving. Look for dishes with fresh vegetables, lean proteins, and whole grains. Identify modifications you can request, like swapping fries for a side salad or opting for olive oil instead of butter.

2. Ask for Customizations

Don't hesitate to request changes to your order. Most restaurants are happy to accommodate dietary preferences—whether that means asking for dressings on the side, skipping cheese, or requesting grilled rather than fried items. Clear communication ensures you stick to your plan.

3. Choose Anti-Inflammatory Ingredients

Look for meals featuring ingredients like salmon, avocado, quinoa, greens, or olive oil. Soups, grain bowls, and salads are often safer choices. Avoid dishes heavy in refined carbohydrates, fried foods, or processed sauces.

4. Be Mindful of Portions

Restaurant servings tend to be larger than necessary. Consider sharing an entrée, boxing half the meal for later, or ordering smaller plates. This helps prevent overeating and keeps portions in line with your goals.

5. Avoid Sugary Drinks

Beverages like sodas, sweetened teas, and cocktails can sneak in unwanted sugars and calories. Opt for water, herbal tea, or sparkling water with lemon to stay hydrated without compromising your efforts.

6. Practice Mindful Eating

When dining out, slow down and enjoy the meal. Being present helps you tune in to hunger cues, preventing overindulgence. Savor the flavors and textures while focusing on the company and experience.

Eating out doesn't need to disrupt your progress. With preparation, intentional choices, and clear communication, you can enjoy meals outside the home while continuing to support your health goals.

Part VI: Resources & FAQs

- 1• Frequently Asked Questions

Transitioning to an anti-inflammatory diet often raises several questions. Below are common inquiries to help guide you through the process with clarity and confidence.

1. What is the main purpose of an anti-inflammatory diet?
The goal is to reduce chronic inflammation by focusing on whole foods such as vegetables, fruits, lean proteins, healthy fats, and whole grains. It helps manage conditions like arthritis, heart disease, and autoimmune disorders while promoting overall well-being.

2. How long does it take to see results?
Improvements in energy levels and digestion may appear within a few weeks. However, long-term benefits, such as reduced joint pain or improved biomarkers, may take a few months depending on individual health conditions.

3. Can I follow this diet if I have food allergies?
Yes, the anti-inflammatory diet can be customized. Gluten-free, dairy-free, vegan, or other allergen-free adaptations are entirely possible. Focus on anti-inflammatory ingredients that align with your dietary needs, such as quinoa, legumes, or plant-based alternatives.

4. Do I need to eliminate all sugar and processed foods?
While it's recommended to minimize refined sugars and processed foods, occasional indulgences are acceptable. Balance is key—try to choose natural sweeteners, like honey or maple syrup, and limit ultra-processed snacks.

5. Is coffee allowed on this diet?
Yes, coffee can be included in moderation, as it contains antioxidants that may offer anti-inflammatory benefits. However, excessive consumption or sugary additives should be avoided to maintain balance.

- 6. What are some quick snacks for busy days?
- Options like roasted chickpeas, trail mix, hummus with veggie sticks, or apple slices with almond butter are easy, nutritious snacks that align with the anti-inflammatory principles.

7. How do I stay on track when eating out?
Focus on meals featuring vegetables, lean proteins, and healthy fats. Ask for dressings on the side, avoid fried foods, and substitute refined carbs with whole-grain options when possible.

8. Can I lose weight on this diet?

Weight loss is often a natural outcome for many, as the diet emphasizes nutrient-dense foods while reducing sugar and unhealthy fats. However, the primary goal is to reduce inflammation and promote better health.

9. What if I experience cravings for unhealthy foods?
Cravings are normal, especially in the beginning. Prepare healthier alternatives, like dark chocolate or sweet potato fries, to satisfy cravings without derailing progress.

10. How do I measure success beyond the scale?
Track improvements in sleep quality, mood, digestion, and energy levels. A reduction in inflammation-related symptoms, like joint pain or fatigue, is also a sign that the diet is working.

These answers offer a roadmap to help you overcome common concerns, empowering you to stay motivated and informed throughout your journey.

2. Supplements and Tools to Support Inflammation Management

While an anti-inflammatory diet forms the foundation for reducing chronic inflammation, certain supplements and tools can enhance the process. These additions, when used wisely, complement a balanced lifestyle aimed at managing inflammation effectively. Below is a breakdown of helpful supplements and tools for long-term support.

Key Supplements for Inflammation Relief

1. Omega-3 Fatty Acids
Found in fish oil, Omega-3 are known for their ability to lower inflammatory markers. Regular supplementation can benefit heart health, joint pain, and cognitive function.

2. Turmeric (Curcumin)
Curcumin, the active compound in turmeric, is a powerful anti-inflammatory agent. Since curcumin has low bioavailability, it's often paired with black pepper (piperine) to enhance absorption.

3. Vitamin D
Adequate levels of vitamin D are essential for immune regulation. Low vitamin D has been linked to increased inflammation, so supplementation can support overall immune health.

4. Probiotics
A healthy gut microbiome plays a crucial role in controlling inflammation. Probiotic supplements with strains like Lactobacillus and Bifidobacterium promote a balanced microbiome.

5. Magnesium
Magnesium supports muscle relaxation, reduces stress-related inflammation, and helps maintain stable blood pressure. Many people are deficient in magnesium, making supplementation beneficial.

6. Boswellia Serrata (Frankincense)
This herb has been used in traditional medicine for centuries to reduce inflammation, especially in cases of arthritis and joint discomfort.

Helpful Tools and Devices for Inflammation Management

1. Foam Rollers and Massage Tools
Regular self-massage using foam rollers or handheld devices can relieve muscle tension and reduce inflammation caused by physical stress.

2. Anti-Inflammatory Tracking Apps
Apps like MyFitnessPal or Chronometer allow you to track your food intake, ensuring you stay consistent with anti-inflammatory meals and supplements.

3. Air Purifiers
Chronic exposure to airborne pollutants can trigger inflammatory responses. Investing in an air purifier ensures a cleaner environment, reducing potential allergens and toxins.

4. Infrared Saunas
Infrared heat therapy can promote circulation and reduce inflammation at a cellular level. It also encourages detoxification, which may benefit those with chronic pain or autoimmune conditions.

5. Blue-Light Blocking Glasses
Chronic exposure to blue light from screens can disrupt sleep patterns and promote inflammation through stress hormones. Blue-light blocking glasses help protect your sleep cycle.

Incorporating these supplements and tools thoughtfully can complement dietary efforts, providing additional support in managing inflammation. Always consult a healthcare provider before starting new supplements to ensure they align with yo
ur individual health needs.

3• Glossary of Anti-Inflammatory Foods

Understanding the key ingredients that promote an anti-inflammatory lifestyle can help you make mindful choices. Below is a detailed glossary of foods known to reduce inflammation and support overall health.

1. Berries
Blueberries, strawberries, and raspberries are packed with antioxidants, especially anthocyanins, which help combat inflammation and oxidative stress.

2. Fatty Fish
Salmon, mackerel, and sardines are rich in omega-3 fatty acids, which lower inflammatory markers and improve heart and joint health.

3. Leafy Greens
Vegetables like spinach, kale, and Swiss chard are loaded with vitamins and minerals, including magnesium, which help regulate inflammation.

4. Turmeric
Curcumin, the active compound in turmeric, has powerful anti-inflammatory and antioxidant properties. It works best when combined with black pepper to enhance absorption.

5. Extra Virgin Olive Oil
This oil contains oleocanthal, a compound that mimics the effect of anti-inflammatory drugs. It also supports cardiovascular health.

6. Avocados
Avocados are a good source of monounsaturated fats, fiber, and essential antioxidants that reduce inflammatory responses.

7. Green Tea
Rich in polyphenols, particularly technically (EGCG), green tea helps lower inflammation and supports metabolic health.

8. Nuts and Seeds
Almonds, walnuts, chia seeds, and flaxseeds offer healthy fats, fiber, and antioxidants, making them excellent additions to an anti-inflammatory diet.

9. Whole Grains
Quinoa, brown rice, and oats are complex carbohydrates with fiber that promote gut health and stabilize blood sugar levels, preventing inflammatory spikes.

10. Cruciferous Vegetables
Broccoli, cauliflower, and Brussels sprouts contain sulforaphane, a compound that may reduce inflammation and protect against chronic disease.

11. Garlic and Onions
Both contain sulfur compounds that enhance immune function and fight inflammation. Garlic also has antibacterial and antiviral properties.

12. Ginger
Ginger's bioactive compounds, such as gingerol, have anti-inflammatory effects and help relieve muscle pain and soreness.

13. Dark Chocolate
High-quality dark chocolate with at least 70% cocoa contains flavonoids, which reduce inflammation and improve heart health.

14. Legumes
Chickpeas, lentils, and black beans are fiber-rich foods that promote gut health and help lower chronic inflammation levels.

15. Tomatoes
Tomatoes are rich in lycopene, an antioxidant that reduces inflammation, particularly in conditions like heart disease. Cooking tomatoes increases lycopene availability.

16. Sweet Potatoes
These are an excellent source of beta-carotene and other antioxidants, supporting immune function and reducing inflammation.

17. Mushrooms
Varieties like shiitake, maitake, and reishi have anti-inflammatory properties due to their bioactive compounds and polysaccharides.

18. Beets
Beets are packed with nitrates, which help reduce inflammation and improve blood flow. They are particularly beneficial for cardiovascular health.

19. Fermented Foods
Yogurt, kimchi, sauerkraut, and kefir are rich in probiotics, supporting gut health and reducing systemic inflammation.

20. Citrus Fruits
Oranges, lemons, and grapefruits provide vitamin C, a powerful antioxidant that supports immune function and helps control inflammation.

This glossary offers insight into foods that work synergistically to reduce inflammation, promote vitality, and enhance long-term health. Incorporating these ingredients into your diet can build a solid foundation for sustained well-being.

4• Recipe Index

A well-organized recipe index makes it easier for readers to explore and plan meals. For an anti-inflammatory cookbook, the index serves as a reference guide, categorizing dishes by meal type, ingredients, and dietary preferences. Below is an example of how the index could be structured to balance clarity and usability:

Breakfasts

•Turmeric Oatmeal with Blueberries

• Avocado Toast on Sprouted-Grain Bread

• Green Smoothie with Spinach and Chia Seeds

• Cinnamon-Roll Overnight Oats

Snacks and Small Bites

• Roasted Chickpeas with Sea Salt

• Apple Slices with Almond Butter

• Trail Mix with Nuts, Seeds, and Dark Chocolate

Salads and Soups

• Quinoa and Kale Salad with Lemon-Tahini Dressing

• Tomato Gazpacho

• Lentil Soup with Spinach

• Roasted Beet and Arugula Salad

Main Dishes

• Buddha Bowl with Tofu and Brown Rice

• Baked Salmon with Lemon and Dill

• Chickpea and Sweet Potato Curry

• Chicken Stir-Fry with Broccoli

Sides

• Roasted Brussels Sprouts with Balsamic Glaze

• Steamed Asparagus with Olive Oil

• Cauliflower Rice Pilaf

Desserts

Chia Seed Pudding with Mango

Avocado Chocolate Mousse

Baked Apples with Cinnamon

Dark Chocolate Almond Bark

This structure offers a balance between accessibility and variety. Each category focuses on recipes aligned with the anti-inflammatory philosophy, helping readers find inspiration based on their needs and preferences.

Conclusion

Embarking on an anti-inflammatory lifestyle is more than just changing the foods you eat—it's about fostering a deeper connection to your health. This book has provided the tools to make that shift manageable and enjoyable, from understanding the role of inflammation in chronic conditions to mastering meal planning and discovering flavorful, nutrient-rich recipes. Whether your goal is to reduce pain, boost energy, or simply feel better each day, small, intentional changes can have profound long-term benefits.

The journey to health doesn't require perfection but consistency. This book encourages flexibility, empowering you to adapt recipes and routines to fit your unique lifestyle. Handling challenges like cravings, dining out, or family meals becomes easier with practice, patience, and thoughtful preparation.

Ultimately, this guide offers more than dietary advice—it lays the foundation for sustainable habits that support wellness for years to come. With every nutrient-packed meal, batch-cooked dish, and mindful choice, you are building a future of vibrant, inflammation-free living. Your journey has just begun, and with the knowledge and inspiration from this book, you're well-equipped to embrace it fully.

78

Made in United States
Troutdale, OR
12/29/2024

27397858R00048